Fed Up

UNIVERSITY PRESS OF FLORIDA

Florida A&M University, Tallahassee
Florida Atlantic University, Boca Raton
Florida Gulf Coast University, Ft. Myers
Florida International University, Miami
Florida State University, Tallahassee
New College of Florida, Sarasota
University of Central Florida, Orlando
University of Florida, Gainesville
University of North Florida, Jacksonville
University of South Florida, Tampa
University of West Florida, Pensacola

Fed Up

The High Costs of Cheap Food

Dale Finley Slongwhite

Foreword by Jeannie Economos

University Press of Florida
Gainesville
Tallahassee
Tampa
Boca Raton
Pensacola
Orlando
Miami
Jacksonville
Ft. Myers
Sarasota

A Florida Quincentennial Book

Copyright 2014 by Dale Finley Slongwhite
All rights reserved
Printed in the United States of America on acid-free, recycled paper

This book may be available in an electronic edition.

19 18 17 16 15 14   6 5 4 3 2 1

Library of Congress Cataloging-in-Publication Data

Slongwhite, Dale Finley, 1951–
Fed up : the high costs of cheap food / Dale Finley Slongwhite ;
foreword by Jeannie Economos.
pages cm
Includes bibliographical references and index.
ISBN 978-0-8130-4984-7
1. African American agricultural laborers—Florida—History.
2. Agricultural laborers—Florida—History. 3. African Americans—
Florida—History. 4. Food industry and trade—Florida—Employees.
5. Food supply—Social aspects. I. Economos, Jeannie. II. Title.
HD1527.F6S59 2014
331.6'396073075924—dc23
2013047859

The University Press of Florida is the scholarly publishing agency
for the State University System of Florida, comprising Florida
A&M University, Florida Atlantic University, Florida Gulf Coast
University, Florida International University, Florida State University,
New College of Florida, University of Central Florida, University of
Florida, University of North Florida, University of South Florida, and
University of West Florida.

University Press of Florida
15 Northwest 15th Street
Gainesville, FL 32611-2079
http://www.upf.com

To the farmworkers of Lake Apopka, living and deceased, who worked tirelessly to plant, harvest, pack, and ship produce all over the country while enduring scorching sun, driving rain, pesticide spraying, snakes, rats, injuries, substandard housing, and low wages.

Maybe stories are data with a soul.

Brené Brown

Contents

Foreword

In 1996, when I first started working for the Farmworker Association of Florida, my job description listed helping write grants and working on Lake Apopka. Little did I know that Lake Apopka would play a major role in my life over the following decade and a half. This included a period of burnout during which I threw up my hands in exasperation and exhaustion and walked away from it all.

For three years, I worked at a botanical garden, spending my days amid the blossoms and butterflies. Even then, I would leave that idyllic setting and travel back to Apopka to participate in community meetings, demonstrations, and even independent research. I could not escape it: Lake Apopka had become my calling, and I had to go back. It was the community; it was the farmworkers. We had started something together. How could I leave it unfinished?

Most people living outside of Central Florida have never heard of Lake Apopka. Sadly, many people living just miles and minutes away from the lake do not know about it. Those who do have heard only vague stories about pollution inhibiting boating and fishing on this lake that was once renowned for its spectacular bass fishing. There are those, mostly locals, who remember the bird deaths in the winter of 1998–99 and the mouse epidemic that plagued the area after the farms closed in '98. Even fewer still remember strange stories of two-headed alligators and fish kills on the lake.

It is rare indeed to find anyone who has heard about or even thought about the people—the farmworkers—who worked in the fields doing

Jeannie Economos presenting a toxic tour of South Apopka. Photo by Gaye Kozanli.

the backbreaking labor necessary to feed a nation. It was for the farm-workers, the people whose voices were lost and shut out in all the talk and plans to clean up Lake Apopka, that I knew I had more work to do. What we started together in 1996 could not be lost. Where that work would take us was yet to be seen. But one thing was certain: this community of people was longing, demanding, needing to be heard. My job, I felt, was to help make that happen.

I first met Dale Slongwhite in 2009 at the Environmental Justice Summit at Barry University Law School in Orlando, Florida. I was speaking on a panel from the collaborators' perspective and Linda Lee was speaking on the panel from the community perspective. It was Linda's first time speaking in a public forum. Geraldean Matthew, who was experienced at public speaking, had dialysis that day and could not attend the event.

As the time for the panel approached, I could tell that Linda was nervous, and I was nervous for her. It was only relatively recently, after all, that Linda, unlike Geraldean—a former Farmworker Association staff member and seasoned public speaker—had become actively involved in Lake Apopka farmworker issues. As Linda would later explain to groups of students on toxic tours, it was the death of her sister Margie that was the catalyst for that change. That day, Linda was summoning all her courage to be an advocate for herself, her family, and her community. As a former farmworker, Linda knew her own story and her own personal experiences. All she had to do was to speak the truth.

And the truth is what moved the audience. Some fifty to sixty people, including academics, lawyers, law students, and professors, applauded loudly when she finished her presentation. Though her talk was hesitating at times and unpolished (she has since become accustomed to and accomplished at speaking to groups and at events), the conference participants were moved both by what she said and the courage it took to say it. She had done it and done it well!

Later that afternoon, as the summit came to a close, people stayed around to talk, network, snack, and discuss the issues. I was gathering our group—Betty Dubose, Earma Peterson, Mary Ann Robinson, Mary Tinsley, and Linda Lee—for the drive back to Apopka. Several people came up to ask questions about the farmworkers and the conditions at Lake Apopka and to express their feelings about what they had learned that day. A lady approached me and told me she was a writer. She said she had been very moved by Linda's story and she wanted to write a book about it. She was fervent, enthusiastic, and sincere. I said, "Sure," and took her contact information.

By this time, like the Lake Apopka farmworkers, I had become used to disappointments and unfulfilled promises. I had been working with the community on the Lake Apopka issue for more than eight years as an employee of the Farmworker Association of Florida and another four to five years in a volunteer capacity. Much like the farmworkers, I was skeptical and a bit jaded by others' enthusiasm and offers of help that never followed through. As I turned away, I thought, "Sure you want to write a book—and I want to win the lottery. I'll believe it when I see it."

Well, seeing is believing. It is five years later, and not only has Dale come through on her promise to write the book but, in devoting her energy, money, and countless hours of her time, she has ensured that the lives and voices of the Lake Apopka farmworker community will be heard and that they will not be forgotten. The result exceeds my wildest expectations. I am thrilled to say that I am—we are—seeing this promise fulfilled! This is a dream come true for me and for the farmworkers, who could not help but wonder whether they and their parts in the Lake Apopka story would be remembered at all. I am forever and deeply grateful that Dale took this project to heart and was unflinching in seeing it through to completion.

The book that you are reading tells a story that you will not hear anywhere else. Dale brings these stories to light and, in so doing, ensures that the people who tell them will live on even after they are gone.

I write this after having gone today to the funeral of former farmworker Betty Woods, whose picture graces the cover. I am sorry that Betty did not live long enough to see the publication of this book, but it is deeply gratifying to know that Betty's story will endure because of Dale's dedicated and tireless work to uncover and gather these stories. To Dale and to the Lake Apopka farmworkers: thank you!

Jeannie Economos
Orlando, Florida

Prologue

In one weekend, Linda Lee attended eighteen funerals. Another weekend, it was thirteen. For years, she and other former farmworkers had been saying that exposure to pesticides on the now-closed muck farms surrounding Lake Apopka had caused their illnesses and killed hundreds of their friends and coworkers.

For decades the farmworkers had inhaled the deadly dust as planes poured pesticides on crops without asking the workers to leave the fields. They had absorbed the poison through their skin during planting, harvesting, and packing, and they had ingested it by eating fish from the canals. Many of them lived a short distance from the farms, so even when they left work after hours of crawling down seemingly endless rows, hacking at lettuce with machetes, or running behind mule trains heaving ears of corn onto pallets, they were not safe. Wind carried the poison to them.

And it wasn't just the farmworkers who were affected. The chemicals used in the pesticides were endocrine disruptors, which means they alter the way the hormonal system works, and this disruption occurs at very low exposures.[1] Extensive research has been done on animals but very little has been done on humans. The farmworkers believe that the high incidence in their children and grandchildren of ADHD, eczema, autism, and other diseases is a result of these pesticides fooling the body into reacting as though it had ingested hormones.

Farm owners[2] insisted they had applied the chemicals in compliance with Environmental Protection Agency (EPA) standards. The EPA was using the best science at the time when they approved the pesticides for use on the fields. Farmworkers had labored on multiple muck farms over the years as well as in other area industries, such as orange groves, ferneries, and nurseries. Each farm used numerous chemicals. Specific illnesses could not be linked to a particular chemical used on a specific farm. No one wanted to take responsibility. Fingers pointed outward, as if waiting for the last of the farmworkers to die and take the whole nasty situation with them to their graves.

*　　*　　*

I first met the Lake Apopka farmworkers in October 2009 when my daughter, Karen, invited me to attend the first annual Environmental Justice Summit at Barry University's Dwayne O. Andreas School of Law in Orlando, an event she was helping organize. I did not even know what the term "environmental justice meant",[3] but I attended as a show of support for her efforts to make a positive change in the world.

Of all the panelists who spoke that day, most touching to me were the former farmworkers of Lake Apopka. Until that day, I had no idea nor had I given much thought to what it took to harvest our fruits and vegetables. I did not know that workers were sprayed with toxic chemicals as they bent over row after row after row in temperatures over one hundred degrees; that these same people went home to a neighborhood housing toxic dumps, a medical waste incinerator, a firefighting range, and other industries with cancer-producing by-products; and that their neighborhood was a mere ten-minute drive from my gated community.

For the first time, I understood that assaults on the environment affect low-income people more than they do the middle class and that the upper class is far removed from the problem. I learned that in the United States, race is the biggest factor when it comes to exposure to lead and harmful pesticides and to the location of municipal landfills and incinerators, abandoned toxic waste dumps, and Superfund sites.[4]

The stories of the farmworkers haunted me for over a year until I could no longer sit on the sidelines. I'm not a lawyer, so I can't fight a legal battle. I'm not a physician, so I can't administer health care. I'm not a scientist, environmentalist, or lobbyist. But there is one skill I do have, and that is what converted me from observer to participant: I have the gift of words. I could craft stories to pique the interest of educators, environmentalists, sociologists, historians, and linguists; I could inform people involved with issues like government, migrant labor, slavery, multiculturalism, and the justice system. I could put faces on the problem.

I approached Jeannie Economos, the pesticide health and safety project coordinator with the Farmworker Association of Florida (FWAF), based in Apopka, and suggested this book. She arranged the interviews, reviewed each story, facilitated a toxic tour of the area, and kept me on track during the project.

I spent hours in the homes of the local former farmworkers and journeyed to meet those who had migrated to farms three hours south in an agricultural area called Indiantown. I listened as they told me about their lives; I transcribed hours of taped interviews; I worked with a photographer who captured the essence of each individual; and I crafted their words into stories.

The full impact of the project did not hit me until I returned to each home to read back what I had written. More than once, the individual nodded as I read and said, "You got that right" or "mm hmm." When I completed the reading, their eyes shone. Some cried. They gave me a firm embrace and tentatively asked if they could have a copy. They knew that I had heard them, and I knew that I was giving voice to those whose voices had not been heard.

And in the process, I learned that what happened on the farms surrounding Lake Apopka is not a "local issue," as some purport. The use of endocrine-disrupting chemicals, the exploitation of those willing to harvest our food, and the targeting of low-income neighborhoods to warehouse toxic waste and toxin-producing businesses is the way America operates.

In my presence, someone asked Jeannie Economos why the Farmworker Association didn't just train the farmworkers for other jobs. I'd been wondering the same thing and waited eagerly for her reply. "Because," she said, "our goal is to add dignity and respect to the profession. Farmwork is a job that is necessary to all of us—we all need to eat. It is also a skilled job. But people should not be made to suffer as a result of being an agricultural laborer, a farmworker."

Today, I chop lettuce with reverence; I offer grace and thanksgiving before meals not only for the food but also for the people who harvested it. When I butter an ear of corn, I remember a little girl sending crates down the chute of the mule train. I know these people now—the farmworkers who crawled on their hands and knees through muddy fields twelve hours a day, six or seven days a week for thirty years to bring this food to me.

My hope is that readers of this book will never again take for granted the crunch of a carrot, the succulence of an orange, or the sweetness of a raspberry—and that they will not only bless the food when they sit down to eat but also remember the farmworkers who brought them this bountiful blessing.

Abbreviations

ADHD	Attention Deficit Hyperactivity Disorder
ANA	antinuclear antibody test
EPA	Environmental Protection Agency
FOLA	Friends of Lake Apopka
FWAF	Farmworker Association of Florida
INS	Immigration and Naturalization Service
PAN	Pesticide Action Network
PANNA	Pesticide Action Network of North America
POPs	persistent organic pollutants
PPT	Permanent People's Tribunal
SJRWMD	St. Johns River Water Management District
TCC	Tower Chemical Company
UFW	United Farmworkers

Chronology

1842	White men settle the land.
1880s	African Americans begin arriving in the Lake Apopka area in search of work after slavery is abolished.
1908–17	James W. "Sawgrass" Jones and Arthur King begin farming the shores of Lake Apopka.
1922	Discharge from the citrus-packing process begins entering the lake.
1917–40	Hopeful farmers come and go from the area.
1937	Lake Apopka passes an ordinance prohibiting African Americans from living or owning businesses north of the Orlando/Tavares railroad tracks.
1941	Apopka passes the vagrancy law.
1941	The state of Florida gives away thousands of acres of wetlands along the north shore of Lake Apopka to encourage muck farming.
1941	The Florida legislature creates the Zellwood Drainage and Water Control District and authorizes the district to drain the marsh. A series of levees and pumps are installed, exposing twenty thousand acres of fertile muck.
1942	Farms begin discharging into the lake.

1947	Lake Apopka is described as a clear-water lake. More than two dozen fish camps circle the shore.
1941–98	As many as thirty-five farms thrive on the north shore of Lake Apopka.
1947	Farmers begin using DDT to eradicate earworms that are destroying crops.
Mid-1940s	Farmers begin using toxaphene and chlordane for pest control.
1962	Rachel Carson publishes *Silent Spring*, warning of the dangers of DDT.
1965	Fishing for catfish is halted due to high levels of DDT in the fish.
1968	Ordinance restricting where African Americans can live and own businesses is rescinded.
1975	DDT is banned in the United States as a possible human carcinogen.
1980–81	Scientists document 1,200–2,000 alligator sightings in Lake Apopka each night.
1985	Lake Apopka Restoration Act passes. The state approves $2.2 million for feasibility studies to help decide which actions are best for cleaning up the lake.
1988	Chlordane banned in the United States on the basis of its being a possible human carcinogen.
Late 1980s	Scientists document 150 alligator sightings in Lake Apopka each night.
1996–98	The state spends more than $100 million to purchase and close the farms to stop lake pollution.
1996–98	Because of the state and federal buyout of the muck farms around Lake Apopka, 2,500 farmworkers lose their jobs.
Fall 1998	In order to begin Lake Apopka's restoration, the fields are flooded in the fall rather than in the spring for the first time in fifty years.
1998–99	One thousand birds die on the shores of Lake Apopka during the migration season.

2000	A $1 million study reveals the birds died from ingesting DDT, toxaphene, and dieldrin.
2000	When farmworkers learn the results of the bird death study, they begin asking for a health study to determine the causes of their many maladies and the deaths of many friends and relatives.
2011	Funding of $500,000 earmarked for the health clinic in South Apopka passes the state house and senate only to be line-item vetoed by Governor Rick Scott.
2011	The Permanent People's Tribunal holds a trial in Bangalore, India, in which Lake Apopka farmworkers are listed as one of twenty-five plaintiffs around the world who have experienced a human rights violation related to pesticide poisoning.
2012	The Florida House and Senate once again approve $500,000 in funding for the South Apopka health clinic. Scott line-item vetoes it.
2012	The Permanent People's Tribunal issues a 274-page report and an indictment against five manufacturers of toxic pesticides and the countries that allow their manufacture.
2012	A representative from the Pesticide Action Network hand delivers a letter to a White House environmental official citing the verdict of the Permanent People's Tribunal.
2012	Senator Barbara Lee of California stands on the floor of the U.S. House of Representatives and speaks on behalf of the Lake Apopka farmworkers.
2012	Orange County commissioner Fred Brummer announces that he wants to add another $1 million to the $4 million the state has already set aside that year to try a new aggressive method for dredging Lake Apopka.
2013	Central Florida leaders outline a plan envisioning Apopka as an eco-village.

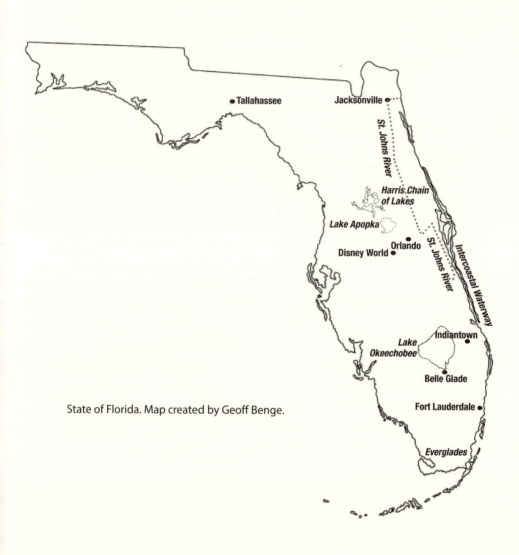

Tallahassee

Jacksonville

St. Johns River

Harris Chain of Lakes

Lake Apopka

Disney World • Orlando

St. Johns River

Intercoastal Waterway

Lake Okeechobee

Indiantown

Belle Glade

Fort Lauderdale

Everglades

State of Florida. Map created by Geoff Benge.

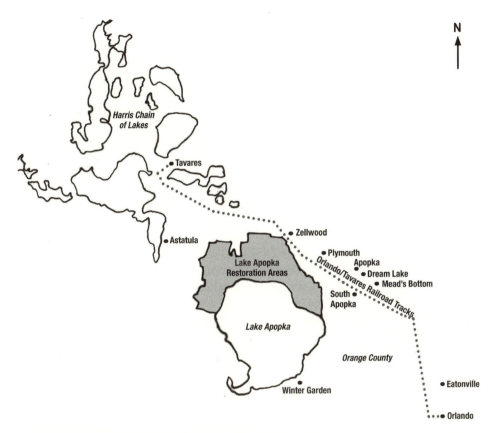

N

Lake Apopka area. Map created by Geoff Benge.

Fed Up

1 *Background of Lake Apopka*

Deadly Assault

In order to understand the farmworkers, we must understand the land. In order to understand the land, we must understand the water. In order to connect the dots, we must understand the animals. In this story, the people, the land, the water, and the animals are forever and inextricably intertwined with the chemicals that poisoned them all.

Three of these groups benefited from millions of dollars spent in an attempt to reverse the damage done by decades of reckless chemical contamination. The people, however, have largely been ignored.

The people of Lake Apopka are more than the labels others have affixed to them—vegetable pickers, farmworkers, laborers, corn harvesters, lettuce cutters, minorities and, later, diabetics, the impoverished, an aging population. They are much more than that. They are American citizens with full lives who labored in the fields to feed the rest of us. Much has been written *about* them. They have been used as statistical data. It's about time we heard *from* them; it's about time we listened *to* them.

Their stories are intimately personal recollections of what life has been and continues to be like for farmworkers in America.

Let's start with the water, move to the land, give voice to the people, and then see how the animals tie it all together.

The Water

Bubbling forth from the pure springs in its southwestern corner, Lake Apopka encompasses just over thirty thousand acres, its waters spreading out to nearly ten by twelve miles.[1] The second-largest lake in the state, Lake Apopka is the headwaters for a series of nine interconnected lakes named the Harris Chain of Lakes.[2]

As recently as 1947, boaters could see to the bottom of the lake.[3] Anglers from around the country were drawn to more than two dozen fish camps encircling her shoreline, where they cast their lines hopefully in popular bass tournaments and fish rodeos.[4] Bird watchers flocked to the area, binoculars dangling from their necks, *Peterson Field Guide to Birds of North America* poking out from their vest pockets. Eagerly they checked off wood storks, great blue herons, snowy egrets, bald eagles, ospreys, and a myriad of migrating species from their life lists.

All the while, rich soil called *muck* percolated on the lake bottom.

The Land

Nearly forty years earlier, in 1908, the Guarantee State Bank of Dallas had attempted to lure Texas farmers to the north shore of Lake Apopka, describing the soil as "Black Gold just waiting for farming prospectors to develop [into] the richest farmland in America."[5] Along with several other men, James W. "Sawgrass" Jones answered the call. Once he saw the potential, he contacted his friend in Tennessee, Arthur King, who arrived late in 1909.[6]

Many farmers became involved in citrus farming and other ventures, but Mr. King attempted to grow vegetables in the marshlands. It soon became apparent that vegetable farming was next to impossible because of a lack of water control. Due to the low level of the land, Lake Apopka frequently flooded the fields.[7] By 1917, Mr. King had given up on what had been touted as the promised land.

Thus began the many years of "suitcase farmers."[8] As one group packed up to leave the area, another group of hopefuls arrived to take their place.

All of this changed in 1941. As the United States' entry into World War II became inevitable, the country looked to ramp up food

A cabbage field on one of the Lake Apopka farms. Photo by Gaye Kozanli.

production on a national level. In a special legislative act in June 1941, the state of Florida gave away thousands of acres of wetlands along the north shore of Lake Apopka to encourage muck farming.[9] The legislature created the Zellwood Drainage and Water Control District and authorized the district to drain the marsh. A series of levees and pumps were installed, exposing twenty thousand acres of fertile muck.[10]

For fifty years, as many as thirty-five large and small farms grew, harvested, packed, and shipped produce all over the country—corn, beans, cauliflower, cabbage, eggplant, celery, carrots, cucumbers, leaf lettuce, artichokes, beets, radishes, and watermelon. New technologies related to freezing, shipping, and processing that were developed on the agricultural lands of Lake Apopka were later adopted worldwide.[11]

Unfortunately, the muck farmers encountered pests that threatened to ruin their crops. One of the first incidents occurred in 1947 when earworms infested the corn. The potent chemical dichlorodiphenyltrichloroethane, more commonly known as DDT, ended the infestation.[12] During World War II, both military and civilian populations had successfully used DDT against mosquitos, which frequently carry malaria and typhus, and it soon became the chemical of choice for insect control in crop and livestock production, commercial and government structures, homes, and gardens. DDT was cheap and effective. Because of the chemical's persistence and versatility, commercial usage of DDT thrived in the United States for nearly thirty years.

Then, in 1962, Rachel Carson published the book *Silent Spring*, warning of the dangers of DDT.[13] The resulting public outcry coaxed the U.S. government into spearheading an intensive investigation of the insecticide. Four government committees issued reports, and in 1972, the EPA banned the use of DDT in the United States, reporting that the chemical was a probable human carcinogen that damaged the liver and the nervous and reproductive systems.[14]

Other pesticides came on the market to take the place of DDT, including toxaphene and chlordane. Like DDT, both of these chemicals are organochlorines, which are persistent organic pollutants (POPs). POPs are toxic chemicals that remain in the environment for a very long time. All POPs used during that era remain in the environment to this day, which is why they are considered "persistent." They adversely affect not only the environment but human health as well. Wind and water transfer POPs from one place to another. As POPs pass from one species to the next through the food chain, they bioaccumulate, meaning they increase in concentration, especially within fatty tissue.[15]

Most organochlorines, including aldrin, endrin, and dieldrin, were banned in the United States during the 1970s and early 1980s even though many were not barred from export to other countries. Chlordane was not banned until 1988.[16] Exposure to this chemical has been associated with cancer, leukemia, and autoimmune diseases.[17]

All the while, tractors sprayed toxaphene, chlordane, and other pesticides on Lake Apopka farms. During the off-season, the levees were adjusted to flood the farmland with lake water as another way to control weeds and pests. When the waters were pumped back into the lake to expose the muck soil for the next season's planting, they brought waves of fertilizer and pesticides into the lake. Wind carried the pesticide dust into nearby homes and labor camps, and over the years, crop dusters dropped tons of the chemicals onto growing vegetables that then made their way to the tables of hungry Americans.

Alongside the north shore of Lake Apopka, fields stretched as far as the eye could see, and way down those rows, blending into the landscape, almost indistinguishable from the plants themselves, were the people—experiencing the same deadly assault as the land, the animals, and the water.

The People

In 1941, around the same time that the use of DDT became popular, Apopka passed a vagrancy law. It was wartime. Men were needed for the army and men were needed on the muck farms, so the town passed an ordinance stating that males aged eighteen or older were not allowed to "loiter on the streets."[18]

Four years earlier, in early 1937, Apopka had passed a law making it illegal for African Americans to live or own businesses north of the Tavares/Orlando/Atlantic railroad tracks. That ordinance held until 1968.[19]

Initially, the people south of the railroad tracks knew nothing of the 1941 vagrancy law. They regularly gathered on the corner of Central Avenue and Ninth Street in front of the Masonic hall to play cards and shoot dice. A cruiser would pull up, and a deputy would inform the "vagrants" of the ordinance, giving them a choice of joining the army, going to jail, or working the muck farms. It didn't matter whether a man was just stopping by to say hello to a buddy. Able-bodied men were needed, and the chief of police knew where to find them.[20]

Most "vagrants" chose the muck farms.

The Water, the Land, and the People

Over the decades, a perfect storm of contaminants converged on Lake Apopka, earning it a designation as the most polluted large lake in the state of Florida. Effluent from a sewage treatment plant in Winter Garden and discharge from Tower Chemical Company (TCC), a pesticide manufacturing plant on the south side of the lake at Gourd Neck Springs, combined to create an environmental nightmare.

TCC disposed of chemical waste in an unlined pond on their property. Due to heavy rainfall in 1979, that pond overflowed into a canal that filtered into Lake Apopka. DDT and other related contaminants were found on the grounds of TCC, in the waters of Lake Apopka, and in groundwater plumes. Eventually, the EPA declared the TCC property a Superfund site.[21]

Phosphorous runoff from fertilizers and pesticides used on farms in the region served as the largest contributing factor to Lake Apopka's pollution. Each year, the area's farms discharged twenty billion gallons of fertilizer-laced water—approximately one-third of the lake's total volume—back into the lake.[22] The fertilizer-induced algae blooms on the lake's surface eventually blocked out the sunlight below. Without sunlight and oxygen, native plants died. Without their food source, oxygen, and habitat, the largemouth bass also died. Between 1950 and 1957, the population of the much-prized largemouth bass dropped from 60 percent of the fish in the lake to 18 percent due in large part to pesticide poisoning and invasive organisms in the water.[23] By 1965, commercial catfish harvesting was stopped because DDT concentration in fish exceeded allowable limits.[24]

The Animals

Alligators

During the 1980s, a team of research biologists from the University of Florida began a study of alligators in the state. Alligator skin is used for leather, and alligator meat is offered on restaurant menus, so harvesting the reptile is a multimillion-dollar industry. Alligator ranchers wanted to know how many alligators could be taken from the environment without harming the population.

In 1980 and 1981, they reported that it was common to see 1,200–2,000 alligators each night in Lake Apopka. By the end of the decade, they found 150 per night.[25] Of course they wondered what could have caused such a dramatic drop in the lake's population.

Alligators typically lay anywhere from thirty to forty-five eggs in a nest. In the wild, about half are expected to hatch. At Lake Apopka, only one-fifth hatched, and half of those died shortly after birth. Further study of the alligators revealed hormonal abnormalities. The penises of the male alligators were substantially smaller than the norm, and the females had misshapen ovaries with multiple eggs rather than the typical single egg. These anomalies had scientists stumped. Only after new research was published did they make the connection between the alligators and endocrine-disrupting chemicals that act like hormones. Since alligators do not wander far from home, the problem necessarily stemmed from changes within their environment.[26]

Dr. Louis Guillette, a reproductive biologist involved in the project since its inception, states that the American alligator "is an important sentinel species to tell us something about the health of the environment." He defines the word "sentinel" as "to watch and warn." In medieval times, sentinels walked the high walls of a city to alert citizens of impending disasters. Sentinel species do much the same for the environment.

"Alligators basically stay within a half-mile of where they were hatched," Dr. Guillette says, "so they are telling you about that spot. They're top predators. They're the ones accumulating contaminants through the whole food chain. You could see effects because they're going to have higher levels than, say, little fish."[27]

Finding himself in a scientific detective story that was to open new directions of research, Dr. Guillette remembers when he began putting the pieces together. "A colleague of mine . . . started talking to us about work he had done and a meeting he had been to that summer, in which he had met Theo Colborn[28] and a number of scientists and said, 'You know, environmental contaminants might be acting like hormones.' And it was all of a sudden, 'Bam!' It was one of these incredible experiences when you realize, I have hormonal abnormalities. I have possibly a contaminated lake. I know I have a top predator that accumulates contaminants, and then it all just kind of came together as a hypothesis."[29]

In the 1980s, this research and these scientific theories were new and groundbreaking. Some environmental scientists accepted Dr. Guillette's work while other scientists scoffed at it. Two decades later, in 2011, he won the prestigious Heinz Award and came to be recognized internationally for his seminal research on endocrine-disrupting chemicals.[30]

According to Dr. Guillette, on the cellular level, an ovary or a testis in an alligator is fundamentally the same as in a human being. When we see an abnormality in an ovary in a contaminated area, it is a red flag and we need to begin testing girls and women. He also says that scientists used to think that reproduction only had to do with genetics, what a person inherits from his or her parents; now there is greater awareness that environmental contaminants are a major contributing factor.[31]

Unaware of the health hazards, the farmworkers continued to catch fish and turtles from contaminated Lake Apopka and bring them home for dinner.

According to the EPA, consumption of fish and wildlife is the primary way humans are exposed to persistent and bioaccumulative toxins. Consumption and use of contaminated fish is an especially pressing concern for many communities of color, whose members may consume fish, aquatic plants, and wildlife in greater quantities than does the general population.[32]

The Birds

Another wildlife tragedy hit the area after the farms were closed in May 1998. (The closing of the farms is discussed at length in the next section.) During the migration seasons of 1998 and 1999, nearly one thousand birds died on the north shore of Lake Apopka. For the first time in more than fifty years, the former Lake Apopka farmlands were flooded during the fall rather than the summer in order to begin restoring the north shore to shallow marshlands.[33] Waterfowl migrating southward saw an expansive and inviting marshy area and decided it would make a good winter home. What they didn't see was the abundance of contaminants in the fish dwelling in and near the irrigation canals. What they had hoped would be a tasty dinner ended up being lethal. Eighty percent of the birds that died were American white pelicans.[34] The others were fish-eating predators and wading birds, including wood storks and bald eagles.

The National Audubon Society described the dying birds as "convulsing and bleeding from the eyes and beak," exhibiting "symptoms of pesticide poisoning."[35]

A few pelicans were found as far away as Mississippi and the Midwest, yet they were linked to Lake Apopka.[36] Organochlorine pesticides reside in the fatty tissue of the body. When affected birds migrate, they use their stored fat reserves, releasing toxins into their bloodstream. Through a $1 million study, the U.S. Fish and Wildlife Services determined that the birds were poisoned by eating fish contaminated with DDT, toxaphene, and dieldrin.[37]

Although the *Orlando Sentinel* reported, "No one is arguing that the off-site bird deaths are unrelated to the Lake Apopka pesticides," there is still a debate over what caused the illnesses of the former farmworkers and their families.[38]

Restoration and Restitution

Restoring Lake Apopka

After years of fretting over what to do with Lake Apopka, the state of Florida passed the Lake Apopka Restoration Act of 1985.[39] The lake had become an eyesore and embarrassment to local communities who wanted a clean image to present to tourists. The state approved $2.2 million for feasibility studies to help decide which actions, among the many proposed, would be the best to clean up the lake.[40] All the options either cost too much or presented significant logistical challenges. Nothing was done except a futile attempt to regulate the farmers and to control the amount of phosphorous runoff from their farmlands.

With urgent prompting from the Friends of Lake Apopka (FOLA), an environmental group committed to restoring the lake and its surrounding wetlands, and the St. Johns River Water Management District (SJRWMD), Florida state representative Bill Sublette prepared a bill in early 1996 that would have enforced a strict pollution cap on farm runoff. When the farmers heard about the proposal, they said they would rather be bought out than operate with the regulatory caps; therefore, in 1996, the state passed the second Lake Apopka Restoration Act, which provided funding to begin buying back the farmland it had given away fifty years before.

By 1998, with funding from state and federal sources, the state had spent in excess of $100 million to purchase the farms, including the infrastructure and farm equipment.[41]

In the process, an estimated 2,500 farmworkers lost their jobs.[42] Counting the spouses and children of these farmworkers, thousands of people were deeply affected. Many lived in shanties provided by the farm owners, in company-owned labor camps, or on farm property in ramshackle trailers they were still making payments on. Among those who lost their jobs was a large population of African Americans who were longtime residents of Apopka and surrounding municipalities.

As part of the buyout, legislators decided to auction off the farm equipment and allocate the proceeds to the local governments—the city of Apopka, Orange County, and Lake County. Only after advocacy on the part of FWAF did legislators give any thought to the plight of the soon-to-be-unemployed farmworkers. A small percentage of the total from the sale of farm equipment was designated for retraining and re-employing farmworkers.[43]

Unfortunately for the farmworkers, some farm owners bought back their own equipment at a fraction of the cost the state paid for it. In addition, the program did not get up and running until after the crop season had already ended. By this time, a significant number of Hispanic workers had left the area for the summer months to harvest crops in other states. When they returned to Lake Apopka in the fall, their jobs were gone. Needing immediate work, many were swept up by the construction and landscaping industries during the housing boom of the late '90s and early 2000s.

Five years later, Orange County had spent only one-third of the money, and much of that went to community centers instead of directly to the farmworkers.[44] For the permanent residents of Apopka, especially the older African American farmworkers, the retraining options proved both unhelpful and unrealistic. Men and women in their fifties, sixties, and even seventies and eighties who had performed farmwork all their lives did not have the skills or physical capacity to do the types of jobs that were offered under the program.[45] Gone was their livelihood, along with the only way of life their families had known for several generations. Gone, too, was their health.

Restitution

When the birds died in late 1998, the farmworkers became extremely nervous. The EPA spent $1 million on a study to determine the cause of the deaths. The results of that study were not published until 2000. The study concluded that the deaths had occurred from ingesting pesticide-contaminated fish. "What about us?" the farmworkers asked. "We were exposed to the same chemicals. We eat fish from the lake."[46]

Once the EPA had linked the bird deaths to high levels of pesticide exposure, the farmworkers began to clearly articulate what they wanted: an official health study to determine whether the chemicals found in the birds were present in significant amounts in their own bodies. If so, they wanted to know what that would mean for their health. They had valid questions, and they were seeking real answers.

"We are human beings," said Tirso Moreno, cofounder of FWAF. "Nothing has been done to protect human beings. We deserve attention, and we deserve that our government will take care of our needs and protect its people."[47]

As the years passed and no health study was forthcoming in spite of attempts by FWAF and some state university researchers to get federal funding, men and women became ill. Many passed away. Hope for a health study dimmed, replaced by the obvious need and urgent demand for health care. Because of the complex and multiple chronic health problems people were experiencing, they needed care that would include specialist attention and medication.

To this day, the community would still welcome a health study, one that would test them for endocrine-disrupting pesticides—but so much time has passed, and so many people have died. They don't want to lose more friends, neighbors, and family members. They are asking for someone to hear their voices so that they can get the health care they so desperately need.

Farmworkers Advocate for Themselves

And so the farmworkers, who had spent their lives bent over the earth following orders from crew leaders and farmers, stood up and advocated for themselves. They held community meetings, asking lawmakers to come hear their cause. They formed a task force. They asked, without much success, to participate in committees with the officials who were making decisions that directly impacted their lives. They took their issues to the media and spoke in front of news cameras that broadcast their situation across Central Florida. They drove five hours to Tallahassee and back again on the same day to lobby in front of state representatives. At meetings between environmentalists and water managers who gathered to discuss the lake restoration and the farmland cleanup, the farmworkers waved handwritten signs asking, "What about Lake Apopka Farmworkers????" They accepted invitations to step onto platforms at environmental conferences in universities and law schools and, despite their lack of high school diplomas, they relayed their stories to PhDs and JDs.

They created the Lake Apopka Farmworker Memorial Quilt Project, hand-sewing two quilts in memory of individuals who had worked on the muck and since passed away. (See chapter 13.) At long last, in 2011, fifteen years after the farms closed, some acknowledgment of the farmworkers' issues and help for their problems came from Florida state senator Gary Siplin, who proposed allocating $500,000 from the $70 billion state budget to help.[48] The funds were earmarked for the local community health center in Apopka—for years known as the "farmworker clinic"—which mainly provides primary care and a clinic for women and children. Siplin had designed the budget allocation to provide financial assistance to community members to help them obtain medication and access to specialists.

The $500,000 allocation passed both the Florida senate and house. The victory and euphoria were short-lived, however, as Florida governor Rick Scott summarily exercised his line-item veto power and slashed the long-awaited funding.[49] Again in 2012, Senator Siplin proposed a $500,000 allocation that passed the senate and house. Sadly, 2012 saw a repeat of the events of 2011.[50] No state money; no health care.

A milestone occurred in mid-2012. Two impassioned documentary filmmakers arranged a telephone interview between Congresswoman Barbara Lee of California and two former farmworkers—Linda Lee and Geraldean Matthew. The congresswoman was so touched by their stories that in May 2012, she stood in front of the U.S. House of Representatives and spoke for five minutes on their behalf. In her words, the former farmworkers are "unflinching in their advocacy of pesticide awareness through their involvement with the Farmworker Association of Florida." She told House members about the hardships of the farmworkers bent over all day in the stifling Florida sun. She closed her speech by offering "gratitude wholeheartedly to these incredible women, to their community, and to farmworkers across the country—for theirs truly are the hands that feed us."[51]

I was present when five former farmworkers gathered at the Farmworker Association headquarters in Apopka to watch the YouTube video of Barbara Lee's presentation to the House of Representatives. The women all leaned forward, listened attentively, nodded their heads, and interjected with, "She's got that right." Their eyes shone with well-deserved pride, and when the video was over, they spent the next half hour relating stories about their days on the farms. Someone in Washington had heard their stories, and they were pleased.

And finally, Pesticide Action Network (PAN) International took notice. PAN, a global network of more than six hundred organizations in over ninety countries, conducted a four-year investigation to identify communities around the world that had suffered violations of human rights involving pesticide exposure. They brought their findings to the Permanent People's Tribunal (PPT), who held court in Bangalore, India, for three days in early December 2011.[52]

Lake Apopka Today

The efforts to clean up the lake continue to this day. The St. Johns River Water Management District has a mandate to oversee the massive task of restoration and must juggle all the competing interests, oftentimes finding itself between different segments of the public and demands from political leaders.[53]

On July 18, 2012, Orange County commissioner Fred Brummer announced that he wanted to add another $1 million to the $4 million the state had already set aside that year to try a new aggressive dredging method.[54] To dredge the entire lake would cost $800 million, so Brummer proposed dredging only the two boat ramp areas. He said, "It is time we try something or Lake Apopka could be lost."[55]

In June 2013, Orange County evicted the dredging company. The project was supposed to be successfully completed by December 2012; however, water "wrung out using that method proved toxic, according to state officials."[56]

In FOLA's spring 2011 newsletter, FOLA president Jim Thomas writes, "As I look at the lake almost every day, I realize that anyone who isn't familiar with the magnitude of the project may not feel that our efforts have been successful. The lake is still green, but if you had seen it in 1995, it was fluorescent green. Now it is brownish green, and the current data shows progress."

In a summit held on February 8, 2013, Central Florida leaders outlined a plan envisioning Apopka as an eco-village. The concept featured ball fields, a BMX track, a Frisbee golf course, rodeo grounds, equestrian facilities, a wilderness lodge, camping cabins, an environmental center, and trails for hikers and bikers and bird watchers. They hoped these plans, in addition to drawing fishermen back to the lake, would contribute financially to the area.[57]

Alligators and birds have their advocates. The lake attracts the attention and advocacy of environmental groups and local politicians.

But what about the people—the farmworkers, the invisible ones? As the drama of the Lake Apopka cleanup unfolds, they are waiting and watching from the sidelines.

What happened at Lake Apopka serves as a warning to us all. The people who tell their stories on the following pages are sentinels. They jumped off the metaphorical wall and crawled among the enemy of environmental contaminants. For more than fifteen years they have voiced their experiences, yet their words have been ignored by those in power who are more interested in making a profit than in helping the afflicted.

2

"Hard to Believe Unless You Lived through It"

William Gladden

"Drop by any time," Mr. Gladden said when I called him for an interview. Apparently, innumerable others have the same invitation, because every time I "drop by," so does someone else.

Mr. Gladden lives in the same neighborhood where he grew up, on "the other side of the tracks" in South Apopka. He spends his days in an electric wheelchair in his circular driveway chatting with older men in pickups, younger men who bring in his mail, neighbors who deliver meals to him, and people of all ages who happen to walk by.

His grandparents migrated to the area from South Carolina at the turn of the twentieth century. As a young boy, he listened to the stories of old-timers in the community; now that he is in his eighties, his knowledge spans a century and a half. He is considered the neighborhood historian and has jump drives filled with historical columns he has written for the newspaper, the *Apopka Chief*. He writes because he wants young people to know their heritage as residents of South Apopka, which he refers to as the Ghetto, the Black Belt, and Soulville.

Mr. Gladden left Soulville for a period of time to attend Morehouse College in Atlanta and to work with Dr. Mitchell S. Rosenthal, deputy commissioner of New York City's Addiction Services Agency. He served on more than one ship in the navy during the Korean War as head steward to the commanding officer. "The navy was highly segregated at that time," he said. "Regardless of my education, there was only one place for my ethnic group to go—the steward branch. You were a cook or took care of the officers."

For twenty years, he was an administrative manager in citrus groves and has firsthand knowledge of DDT and a product he referred to as Paragon.[1] He says, "Paragon was a very dangerous pesticide that killed quite a few grove workers over a period of ten to fifteen years. It accumulates in your body and you're paralyzed and you are out of it."

Most Negroes migrated into Apopka after Reconstruction by riverboat through the intracoastal waterways. Anywhere from the 1880s on into the 1950s. Right after slavery, most Negroes didn't have anywhere to go. They didn't have much education, or they weren't skilled people. All most of them could do is plant a crop. Sharecropping was a big thing.

Florida was booming. They'd just begun to establish citrus growing, and people came here—what you might say—in droves.

Say a friend was already in Florida. He might have gotten word to the Carolinas or somewhere, "Look, man, come on down here. At least we can live. We can go into farming." It was really networking between groups of people.

They came by boats, little skiffs, any way they could get here. It was cheaper and more accommodations for people to use the waterways than it was to use the trains. A man could put his family on a boat, and his furniture, and come on down here. Practically every state on the East Coast has an intracoastal waterway. You could go in and out, in and out, work your way right on down the line. What played an important part—you have this chain of lakes, you can go from one lake to another, cut through canals, or come down any number of tributaries.

Standard Grove was a citrus grove along Clay Springs north of Apopka. The owners set up this shantytown called Johnsontown. The people would come on down the river, settle in the shantytown, and work in the grove.

My people came here by boat. I could name you numerous people whose families came to Apopka by boat. That's how most people came into this area.

William Gladden. Photo by Gaye Kozanli.

Sarah Mead was one of my people. She came down the rivers by boat and homesteaded the area at the junction of State Road 441 and State Road 436. It was called Mead's Bottom Quarters. She had shanty houses down there, rental shacks. A lot of Negroes lived in that area while they looked for employment, found housing in sharecropping, or in some cases while waiting to purchase homes or farms.

We also had the Longhouse Quarters, named for their shape; the Brown Quarters, also called Foggy Bottom Quarters; the White Quarters, named for their color; the Red Quarters; and the Graveyard Juke Quarters, built for the muck farmworkers who came in for the seasons. The Graveyard Quarters were known from Florida to New York for its irregularities.

Most of the shacks in the Mead's Bottom Quarters were constructed out of pine tree slabs that the planing mill had discarded and let people take for free. Construction usually consisted of one room, occasionally a window, one door, and dirt floors. They were frequently referred to as shotgun houses because they resembled looking down the barrel of a twelve-gauge shotgun.

My uncle Michael Gladden and a brother lived in Mead's Bottom for a while. They recalled lying down in bed and gazing upward to count the stars in the sky. This was because most of the roofs of these homes were not completely closed to the elements.

Now when I came along as a boy in the war years, that's when the muck became real popular. They grew beans out there. Beans were the main crop. Over the period of years, they got into everything that you could get in as far as vegetables were concerned.

My uncle Michael Gladden owned the Gladden Store. It was located at 22 West Ninth Street, but now they call it Michael Gladden Boulevard. People depended upon that store, especially in the '40s. They could get their foods from there, mostly on credit. He trusted them and they trusted him. There's no ifs, ands, or buts about it.

I saw people working on the muck come in there early in the morning, getting ready to go to work. "Look, Mr. G.," they'd say. "Would you let me have some bologna? Would you let me have a loaf of bread? When I come in this afternoon, I'll pay ya. I'll pay ya Friday."

My uncle Michael was an educated man. Both he and my daddy went to Morehouse College. They lived up north until their father's death in

1925. It was my grandfather who started the store, but he left it in great debt, so my uncle Michael and my daddy came back to pay off his debts.

My uncle Michael ran the store. People liked to talk to him. He was a wise man. He could give you advice and what have you. My daddy opened a business, the Shoe Hospital. I used to have to deliver shoes uptown. It was quite an experience. My father's business was 99 percent white rather than my heritage, so I was fortunate enough to have associated myself with people on both sides of the tracks.

Around March of 1937 an ordinance was passed that Negroes could not live above the railroad tracks nor could they own businesses above the railroad tracks. Everybody was supposed to live below the Tavares/Orlando/Atlantic railroad tracks. That ordinance held until 1968 when Leonard Hearst became mayor.

My ethnicity was really afraid of the banks. They did not want the man above the railroad tracks to know what they had, so they would ask my uncle Michael to hold their money for them in the store. "Well, all right, Mr. Gladden, here's $50. Keep it for me." Now that $50 might stay there for a year or overnight he might want it back. Fortunate enough, my uncle was an honest man and he didn't use their money to afford his endeavors or what have you. I've never heard anyone say that he stole from them or he took their monies.

The store closed in the early '70s after some fifty-odd years in business. When we opened the safe that he had during his business years, you would be amazed at what was in it. No money in it, but records. He kept records, and they were there.

I remember when the German prisoners of war were here.[2] They worked on the muck or in the insecticide plant where McDonald's is now. Mr. Grossenbacher, who was the federal agriculture agent at that point in time, brought the war prisoners in during World War II. You'd go up there and you'd see them standing near the wall or mixing certain chemicals and what have you. They didn't bother anybody, and we didn't bother them.

In 1941, Apopka passed a vagrancy law that resulted in Negroes being arrested and put to work on the new muck farms. Fred Reisner was the chief of police during that time, and they didn't want anybody eighteen years old or better loitering on the streets. Nobody below the tracks knew anything about the new law. Reisner and another deputy would come down Michael Gladden Boulevard or Ninth Street and Central Avenue. The Masonic hall was there. It was a wooden building. Everybody hung out there. They would play cards and they would shoot dice right out there near the hall.

The officers would catch these fellows and give them a choice. They'd say, "Well, all right, go to jail, go to the army, or go to work on the muck." Most of them, they'd hit the muckland. All Mr. Reisner had to do was contact the man at the Selective Service board, and he'd have you shipped out of here before you could bat an eye.

It really wasn't profiling or anything like that. I've never known Caucasian persons to hang out like we hang out. The deputies targeted that area for the simple reason they needed people to work in the muck or to fight in the war, and they knew where to find them. They would say, "Now here goes able-bodied men standing on the street corners all day long. We just can't have that. We need these people."

Today there are more Hispanics in the fields than Negroes. The switch came about due to the fact that labor laws changed. There was more protection for African Americans, so they had to reach across the border, get these people, and bring them in. Individuals could come from one country to another just by walking over here. Most of my heritage did not want to do certain works, so therefore you called upon the Hispanics or the races of people that would come for a J-O-B. They came in just about like we came in—uneducated, nowhere to go, and the workforce needed people.

Some things are just hard for you to believe unless you actually have gone through it. Yes, sir.

3 | *"Too Many Funerals"*

Linda Lee

I love to visit Linda Lee. I feel as welcome as the ever-present great-grandbabies she cares for every day—a toddler doing somersaults around her small living room; another crawling up my leg; a baby in a carrier here or there; a kindergartener telling me her dreams of becoming a singer; a middle-school girl fetching things at Linda's request. More children will arrive after school, Linda tells me.

Delicious aromas of collard greens and fried chicken waft in from the kitchen, where the flooring has been stripped away waiting for a grandson to finally replace it. The drone of *Bonanza* reaches us from the television in the corner, and the squeak of a boxed fan hanging in the doorway to a bedroom circulates the humid air.

On one particular visit, Linda was sitting on a daybed in one corner hand-stitching a pillow with three-dimensional brown hands affixed to the top. She hopes to sell them, she told me, to repair the leaking roof now covered with a blue tarp. She was too sick to work on the pillows the Friday before. Head-achy, weak, fatigued. When she spoke to half a dozen friends, they all had the same symptoms. "Must have been something in the air," she said.

Another visit, we sat on steel folding chairs in her driveway of patched tan carpets covering ruts and tree roots. The children had pint-sized chairs they dragged over from a collection near the fence that borders the driveway.

> Beyond the fence is an acre or two of land the city took by eminent domain for $1. I could picture the Sunday family gatherings of Linda's youth in the now "No Trespassing" area—afternoons of baseball and games and laughing and eating food it took the women two days to prepare.
>
> Now Linda is limited by lupus, complications from a kidney transplant, and other maladies. Still she greets me with a smile and "How y'all doin'?"

When I was coming along, it was old people dying. You very seldom seen a baby die or you seen a young person die. It was older people. You go to older people funeral. You never really go to no young people. Now they having more young people and baby funeral than older people. We had a few people die of AIDS, but we had people die of emphysema, lupus, heart attack, heart failure, a lot of people having kidney failure. Stuff like that.

At one point, there was actually eighteen funerals in one weekend; another time, thirteen. It was high numbers. Some of them was anywhere between twenty-two to fifty years old. Passing away.

I'm goin', "Oh my God." I told my daughter, I say, "I'm not cookin' for no more funerals. I'm not sending no more cards. Cuz I'll go totally broke. I just give them my condolences, because you can't spend that much money. Don't have it to spend."

They say that some of the chemicals can't leave your body, so I think it's just passing on in the blood or the genes, and when it gets to another generation, it goes into another stage or whatever. So the kids have a lot of different health problems. The next generation sufferin' with asthma. They on the breathing machines. And they're having eczema. PJ, my great-grandson, he got it real bad. The skin on his little legs is all eat up. I try to keep him oiled down.

I hate to tell the story about how my mama and them got to Apopka. Before they got here, they went through some real hardship.

My grandfather—everybody like to say he was mean. But I didn't see him mean. He was stern. He was the type of person—"You not goin' to use me in any kind of way. I work hard. I put in a good day's work." He'd always say that. "But you not going to come here and try to take what I got." That's why I say they was stern people.

Linda Lee. Photo by Gaye Kozanli.

My mama say they came out of Georgia and moved to Marianna, Florida. They worked up there just like farmwork on this end. They say they had quarters there, little shanty houses, that's what they stayed in.

Mother say one night—I guess it was the time of the season when nobody workin' and makin' no money—this man, he have a wife with a couple of children. He went to the store and he stole a loaf of bread. He say the store owner or whoever come to the quarters that night. They drug the lady out the house and cut the baby out of her. They lynched the lady and the man, cut them up, and burned them.

My mama say my granddaddy seen this and grabbed my grandmother and their three children and they trekked to the railroad track. They hit the railroad track and they walked till they got to Apopka. 320 miles. They walked 320 miles. When they got to Apopka, my granddaddy went to working for the pulp man on A Street.

I guess that's why they always tried to keep us so close-knit. They didn't want nobody to come and penetrate our little world because they was the kind of people who worked for what they got and they didn't want nobody come in and try to do all kind of crazy things.

Childhood

I had a great childhood—a loving mother, father, grandmother, grandfather, aunts, uncles. We were a fabric knit of close people. I sit down sometimes and I remember.

We had a lot of land. My grandfather had land right next to us. Every week, I remember my mom and my grandmother and my aunts start cookin' on a Friday. My mama had gas, but my grandmother had a wood stove. They cooked all kinds of cakes and pies and cookies and different stuff. All kind of meat dishes—beef, pork, chicken. They even had a little 'coon and turtle on the table.

On Sunday evening when we got out of church, we came home and there was like a melting pot at my grandmother's house. Everybody would come and eat and be laughing and have fun. Get out in the field and play softball. That was our thing. Softball. My grandfather never got out there and played, but my grandmother, she was shortstop. My mama couldn't play because she couldn't walk that much. But my aunt would get out there. She'd hit that ball, but she wouldn't run. She'd say, "You'd better run for me."

I think about it. Quite a few people come. My mama, my daddy, my uncles and aunts and cousins. Seventeen of us. Sometimes more.

My grandfather sit in a chair—he didn't get up and move around—but he had a little thing to keep us from doin' things we had no business doin'. He would get us 'round his chair and he'd say, "There go Margarita. There go Old Tom right there."

That's how he kept us in line. He'd get us on one side of the house and say, "You better not go around there because Margarita gonna get you. If you go there, Old Tom, he watchin' you. He watchin' you." He didn't have to whoop us.

We never did realize he was talkin' about the birds until after we got grown. I called my sister. I said, "I know what Papa was talkin' about."

She say, "What?"

I say, "He was talkin' about the birds. You think about it. You ain't never seen nothin' in those trees but birds, did you? They was the birds."

The joyful thing was when my grandfather's sisters came down. We called them the little people. They stood no more than four feet tall. They wore size four and five shoes. They were some hard little women. You couldn't get by them. I thought my grandfather scared us, but they would scare you sho' enough.

They didn't really have to whoop us, but when we did get a whoopin', *we got a whoopin'*. We got a *good* little whoopin'. They always had a way of keepin' you in line with little stuff that sure scared us. They hit somethin' and make a loud noise. You gonna be jumpin' and goin' all over tryin' to figure out what goin' on.

My daddy and my granddaddy used to raise hogs. My daddy raised about one hundred head by hisself. There was just him, my mama, and us. We didn't really see about the hogs, but we tantalize the hogs. I remember in the summertime, he had one hog pen was built around a grapefruit tree. There were some big, old pretty grapefruits on that tree. We would get up and walk the fence and get the grapefruits. Then the hogs go to having piglets.

Us little bad girls, we jumped in there and wrestled the pigs. We say we gonna tie them like they do on TV. Hogtie them. So we was up on the pen one day, and we saw one pig go in a side where he not supposed to be. He snatched a whole ham-size out of another hog, and ever since we seen that, we stopped harassing them pigs. We thought if he do another hog like that, what he do for us! So we stopped wrestling. We just keep up in the tree over the pen in the summertime and eat grapefruits. Sometimes, we'd take the water hose and put it in the pen to keep the hogs from getting dehydrated.

We had chicken pens, and we had our own playhouse. Our daddy built our own playhouse. We got in the yard and we played cookin' collard greens and cookin' cornbread and whoopin' our children with the switch and nursin' our babies.

My grandfather had Prince Edward tobacco. He had those great big old cans. When he was finished with tobacco, we would take them and we would make them rolla packa or stilts. For rolla packa, you take the cans, put sand inside, you run a piece of wire through it, put them soda water tops on it, and when you drag it along the ground, it's gonna make noise. So that was our fun.

And then they would bring the big old barrels off the farm. They were huge drums. Some of those had pesticides in them and some of them used to store different stuff they have out there.

Once you get on those barrels, we little circus girls cuz we could run from one end of the row to the other end of the row. Just walk 'em. Just walk them barrels. I tell the kids now, "You ain't half as good as we was." I say, "When we was a little girl, we play Tarzan, we jump on the trees, we roll on the barrels."

Daddy made us a little pushcart one time and one part of our land slant down off the highway. Boy, we get in that pushcart and down that hill we go. He could make a whistle from a duck feather and we'd blow it all day long.

Pretty much, we kept to our own fun and all. We play hopscotch, jackstones. We did the best we can with what we had. And was happy with it.

My grandmother used to make five gallon buckets of teacakes that last us the whole week. We could go to the store and get a five-cent soda, get us a teacake, and you in heaven.

After my grandfather passed, we kept comin' together on Sundays,

Mule train used in corn harvesting. Photo used by permission of Rafe Parker.

but when the big cheese die, it's never the same. We had fun and all, but you could feel a missin' part with him not being there.

My daddy didn't play no migrant stuff because he had girls and he didn't want his girls on no camps, so we stayed right here in Apopka. My mama say before they went to having children they used to travel, but after she started having those childrens, Daddy say no traveling with the kids.

I started working on the farms at an early age. They have a mule train. It's actually a tractor and it's made with wings on it. It's straight on the front and the ladies stand on it and pack. Above their heads, they put the boxes that come down a chute. The ladies have to reach up and take them down to pack the boxes and put them on the little table they had by them to pack them.

That's what I started doing. I was on top, about twelve feet off the ground, pushing boxes in the chute when I was seven or eight years old. It's a long chute, and when you pushed it, you had to push it hard to make sure it was tight. When you push it and you get a slack in it, you gotta keep feeding the boxes in there because somebody constantly taking them down and packing them.

I did all that in the summertime. That's one thing my parents did stress—that we get an education. Mama made us stay in school. When we was out of school, on holidays, and weekends, we worked. There was always something going on the weekends. They was picking beans or cucumbers or okra, thinning corn. Papa would get a little crew and take us out there. It would get the kids some money to do the things they wanted to do with it.

My mama would have us save our money. Before we went back to school, she'd let us go to Orlando. We'd get a chance to go to the movie. We'd get a chance to buy something for ourselves and buy our school clothes. We bought all our personal needs to last us. If we had some money left over and she needed to pay a bill, we would help her pay the light bill or whatever. Mostly our mama and grandparents wanted us to save. We saved a little. Not a whole lot of saving. Just a little saving.

Adulthood on the Muck

I started in '67 working on the muck and worked till the '80s. We hoed rows of chicory and escarole. We thinned it out. When there's just about three inches outside the ground, we have to make sure there only one plant there so it won't grow funny. It not gonna produce right if you don't thin it out. You had to make sure there was only one in the hole. After you thin it out and it get grown, you go back through the fields and you cut and you pack them in a crate. Once they pack them in the crates, sometime we have women crew and we have to load our own crates on the truck. The men would drive the truck, but they didn't load the truck. No, we packed the boxes and put them on the truck.

The men had a lot of different stuff to do. They sprayed the fields. They went to the packing houses and loaded the boxes at the packing houses. That's where the harder part came in. Loading them up on those trailers.

Sometimes they run them through what they call the pre-cooler. That's where cold water is run over the boxes for a period of time and then they put them in the truck and pack them with ice. I guess it depends on what kinds of vegetables it is, they have to keep it fresh. They pack it with ice and stuff. So the men would do stuff like that.

My grandfather ran a crew on the farm. He had a ladies crew. He had quite a bit of women. He split it up between he and my grandmother.

Some might work in caladium, and some might be working thinning corn or thinning chicory or escarole.

My grandfather was out there on the farm and on the muck all the time—running the crew, getting ice, setting turtle lines—and we went right along with him to play. They had ditches where they irrigated the farm. He would go out there and catch a lot of fish. He set out lines for turtles, and we'd go out there and shake the turtle lines. We were constantly back and forth on the farm doing something.

In '82, I was trying to get my CNA [certified nursing assistant certification], so I worked the fields during the daytime and worked in a nursing home at night. When I worked in the fields, I wasn't on the ground cuttin' nothin'. I left that for somebody else to do. I tried to work in the carrot house. I couldn't work in that carrot house because of the wetness. When you in the carrot house, you wet all day. I mean, that water on the carrots when they wash them, it keep you wet all day. And every time I get wet like that, I get sick, so the doctor told me not to do that. So I tried to figure out what I had to do.

Instead, I checked corn. Checking corn is sitting down with a pad and pencil all day making sure everything was straight going out the field. They got a loader on the back that puts the crates on the truck, crate by crate, and I'm the person that checks every crate that goes off the mule train onto the truck and up to the packing house. We checkin' it so the ladies that's packin' the corn can get paid for the amount of corn they pack. I keep count of everything.

Health

The health thing back then . . . most doctors had a black side and a white side. Black people went in the back door and white ones in the front. Trying to get somebody to treat you in Apopka, mmm mm. We had two doctors. One of them won't see no black people, but the other that seeing you, they had a baby that die in his office. A lady took a baby up there for help and by the time he decided to come down, the baby were dead. So we kind of ruled him out.

One day, we was all in the field, and we were just jiving around. Sometimes to make the time go faster in the field, we would joke around with each other. So we were joking this particular day, and somebody happened to pull out a bottle of Motrin.

I say, "You take Motrin?"

She say, "Yeah."

Then everybody say, "You take those pills?"

I say, "Yeah. I take them for my legs."

We got to talking. One person says, "I take them for my heart." Another for something else.

"Wait a minute here!" I say. "There are at least thirty of us here. We take the same pill, and all of us got something different wrong with us."

I told my sister, I say, "When I go back up there, I'm goin' to ask can I be released to go somewhere else for medical care."

So I end up with pneumonia, so they say. I went to the hospital and stayed there. I came out of the hospital, so I went back to the same doctor for a follow-up.

He told me, "Ain't nothing wrong with you. You overweight. You need to lose weight."

I'm looking at this man. I've been sick and I lost at least forty-five pounds. How skinny he want me? I weigh ninety-eight pounds once, and that no fun because I would catch any door. When that door hitcha, every bone, that hurt. So I was going, I don't want to be skinny skinny no more.

I told him I wanted my papers released so I could go get better care.

He say, "Oh, you gettin' the best care here. I'm not going to release your papers."

I started to crying in the office, so this lady, she was a nurse, she came and said, "Honey, what's the matter?"

I say, "I want my papers. I want to see a better doctor because I don't feel like I'm being treated right."

She said, "All you got to do is sign this thing right here."

I signed it. But before I could start going to the clinic in Orlando, I got sick and fell in my front yard. The guy that liked me, he was coming in the yard this day.

He stopped the car and said, "What's wrong with you, Linda?"

I said, "I don't know. My legs just gave out."

He said, "I'm taking you uptown—"

I said, "NO! You ain't takin' me uptown. Uh uh. Uh uh."

So we went to the hospital in Orlando, Florida Hospital, on Rollins Street. I wasn't over there a good hour before the lady say, "Linda, you know you got lupus?"

I'm looking at her like, "Who got lupus? I ain't claimin' nothin'. I ain't claimin' nothing." I told her *she* might have lupus, but I ain't got it.

But I was in and out of the hospital. Every time I turned around, my legs wouldn't move or my eyes went dim. All kinds of crazy. I wonder, why am I keep winding up at this hospital?

Then I tell the man who liked me, "I want you to do me a favor."

He say, "What?"

I say, "Stop at the library and check out some books on lupus, and we read up on this thing."

So I started reading up on it. I started trying to eat like they say in the books. I've always been a fruit and a vegetable person. All my mama and them land had plums. We had oranges, all kinds of oranges. We had opossum brown, navels, temples, even one called pineapple; we had all kinds of oranges. We had grapefruit, tangerines. I could eat all day with oranges; I loved the oranges.

The thing about it. It make me mad I can't go out the door and pick none off the tree no more because of the lupus. But anyway, I was already eating pretty good. We eat a little pork, true; we had a little beef, too; we had a little chicken. But I never been a good meat eater. I like my fruits and my vegetables. You can give me a banana, apple, orange, or whatever, and I'm satisfied.

Then when I went to reading up on lupus, I'm going, "I'm gonna try to do better."

I went to the doctor one time and they tell me, "You got to eat no tomatoes."

And I'm goin', "That's my first love! I love my tomatoes."

It was hard. I'd look at them and think, "I can't eat them." Then I was a grapefruit eater, too. No grapefruit. I'm going, "JESUS! Everything I like to eat, I can't eat." They say that grapefruit brings the enzymes in your medicine down.

I'm going, "Well, I planted a tree. I've got a tree back there that's full of grapefruit and I can't eat none of it."

I told my neighbors, I say, "I keep it fertilized, but y'all can have the fruit off it. I just grow it."

Been quite a few people work on the muck have lupus. Before I got diagnosed and I knew about lupus, one of my girl's friends she went to school with, she had it. She died before she even got sixteen. She died of lupus. She didn't work on the farm. I think her parents worked on the farm. And then another girl, she worked on the farm sometimes, she passed. She had lupus. Been quite a few people around us that died with lupus.

I think it the pesticides. We actually got sprayed with pesticides in the fields as we were working cutting leaf stuff, cutting chicory and escarole. You done finish a field, and they come through with a tractor spraying it. That stuff, it's a liquid. It's misty. It just comes right over on us.

I have arthritis, had my gallbladder removed, had a kidney transplant, part of my small intestines removed, and my teeth ache lots of the time, but I don't have no cavities.

At one point, I went to Pahokee, near Belle Glade, for three months, because I thought I could work, but I couldn't work in them cane. They would burn off the cane fields for the mens to cut it.

Before they burn the sugarcane, they tell you, "Don't go outside." So I don't go outside. Know how soot is when it fallin' on you? Little black stuff. It would be all over everything. All over the car. All over the house. But I never did go outside because I knew that I was allergic to it. But it still affected me. Every time they burn the cane down there, I had stuff like fish scales on me.

I kept going to the doctor. The doctor told me, "You need to leave this area." I couldn't stay down there.

What they sprayed in Apopka affected my skin, too. But it didn't do me like it did when I went to South Florida. It would be like a rash on my side. But down there, it would be like I had an ashy, scaly something or other. I guess different chemicals affect you in different ways.

Even when we was working on the farm on the weekend, we come home, we take what we call a light bleach bath. You put three caps of Clorox bleach in your water and stroke down to try to keep the muck out of your skin. After you stroke down, you rinse down good, and afterwards, you put on baby oil.

Once muck get in your skin, it do you bad. The muck have the chemicals in it, too. When you look at it, it look like it have crystals or something in it. It look powdery at one point, and then when it dry, you can see like it's got crystal or something. You can actually see it glittering. It would bite and itch you real bad. My grandmother used to keep corn husks and lotion to put on our hands and on our feet, but we cleaned up with baby oil after, also. I guess everybody family did different, but that's the way our family did to get the muck out of your skin.

Workin' People

The farms started closing between 1996 and '98. We wasn't aware that they was selling out. They came along and told us they were ending our jobs, just like that. No warning. Just ended it one day. "Here your money. You can go."

I wasn't out there. My sister Margie out there. She came home, she say, "My job ended today."

You know, we tease a lot of time to make fun. I say, "Stop teasing. Your job ain't ended cuz you know they got all those carrots out there."

She say, "I ain't lying. They gave us our check and send us home."

I say, "You tellin' the truth?"

Some government agency come in and say they was gonna set up programs to reeducate the people. Then I noticed they callin' us to meet, so we went to the meeting to try to figure out what they were goin' to do with the people they laid off.

I hear people say there were people working on the muck who were illiterate. But we weren't crazy. We graduated from high school. We did have a diploma. The muck was like fifteen minutes away from home. And with Mother sick in the bed and with Grandmother—we had to feed her through a tube—we didn't want to go to Orlando to get no job. So we had the younger ones trying to help out at home, and we was trying to work on the muck and all to be close by.

But anyway, they put this money up. They set up these programs. Brought a lot of computers in. Say they was going to teach us computer work. I really wanted to learn computer work. But they didn't have nobody there to teach the classes. How you got a computer you don't know what to do with it? Okay, I turned it on. But now what I do? I gotta play with it. I'm going, "This is crazy."

They said they were going to give farmworkers liberty change. Well, that didn't happen. So we got a lot of people that's on the muck sitting home without a job, couldn't make it because they didn't know where they were going to get their next penny from. Didn't have no program where they were giving out money, didn't have no program where you could work to get some money.

We been working peoples all our life, and we was always taught to do what was right. To help somebody. To help ourselves. I think back to 1978 when all of a sudden we see peoples on our property trying to survey something. We say, "What that man doing out in the field looking at our land through that thing?"

So my sister went out there and she asked. They wouldn't give us no explanations, none. So my brother working for an orange company in Orlando. We called him on the CB radio. "Somebody here on the property. You need to come home to see what going on."

His boss man heard us telling him these people keep coming every day, and every time you see them, you try to ask them something, they won't talk to us. They are on our property, they need to give us an explanation, they not giving it. So his boss man said he'd have his lawyer look into it. Well, they looked into it. The county decided they wanted our property to put in a drainage ditch on it. But how they got it is really hurtful, because like I say, my mama and them paid the taxes. They paid for what they wanted at the store. They did not take from nobody.

The county came and told my parents they were going to depreciate the land to $1. The first time I ever saw my grandmother cry like a baby. She boo hoo cried. She said, "What am I gonna do, gonna do, gonna do."

"Well," I said, "I don't know."

They just cried up something that day.

I rode through town—the white side and the black side. I didn't see no reservoir or retention pond that big on the white side of town that I see on this side of town.

One night they had a meeting, and I turned out to the meeting because I wanted to know why they going to take my mama and them's land. You know what they did when I questioned them? They took their little briefcases, closed them up, and walked out of the building. They sure did that. They didn't want to talk to us no more.

My grandparents walked 320 miles to come and work in Apopka. They had worked hard to save and buy that land. My grandmother lost her mind after they forced her to sell the land for $1. She took to bed and that was that. It make me cry now to even think about it.

Sometime I sit down and talk about these stories. I tell what's true. I don't bite my tongue. But some of it, I don't want to be talkin' about. It's not all about the money to me because money can't take you to heaven, but it can get you to hell.

4

"Not Enough Cheekbones to Hold Your Tears"

Geraldean Matthew

For two years, Geraldean Matthew held the funeral program of a coworker close to her heart. Many mornings, she dialed the phone to share a tidbit of her day forgetting no one would be there to pick up on the other end. She showed me her collection of at least three dozen funeral programs of friends who worked beside her on the muck. There wasn't enough room on the table to display her entire collection, which was tucked safely away in another room.

Geraldean asserts that as far back as 1974, farmworkers knew something was going wrong in the fields. Snakes, rats, and birds lay dead after pesticide spraying. It was customary for mothers to bring children to the fields, and it wasn't uncommon for these children to develop nosebleeds. Itchy blotches appeared on arms, legs, and faces. Older folks needed spit buckets by their beds. Most dared not complain lest they be told, "Don't come to work if you don't like it." As for Geraldean, she would sometimes grab her six children and leave on foot.

Just when I thought her personal stories couldn't get any worse, she'd come out with another one about death, murder, sex, or child labor, stopping between each one to cough up thick phlegm into a tissue. She'd sing, cough, talk, cough, laugh, cough.

For years, she could not afford the medications prescribed to her. As a result, her innumerable ailments

Geraldean Matthew. Photo by Gaye Kozanli.

worsened, and these days, Geraldean spends four hours three mornings a week hooked up to a dialysis machine.

Between dialysis sessions, she gathers up energy to fight for justice. Since the farms closed, she has been a key figure in organizing the farmworkers to lobby for the rights afforded to all other types of labor. As for politicians, she says, "We come out of those fields dirty and sweaty and go straight to the polls to vote for those people. Then we go to Tallahassee to lobby, and they won't even ride in the elevator with us. We hear them say, 'There are those stinkin' farmworkers.'"

Geraldean describes herself as a "big-mouth person" who would get "raving upset and make all kinds of noise" when she witnessed injustice in the fields.

I would have to agree with Geraldean's self-assessment—it stands true to the present time.

We should have known it was somethin'. There'd be snakes that crawled like they wasn't a snake. There'd be turtles on the bank. Birds dead in the field. Rats dead in the field. We used to see all of that, but we never give it a thought as to what could be happening until about 1985.

That's when Linda's cousin jumped off the mule train—a big machine where fourteen women packed corn. They got to the end of the field and she jumped off so she could pee-pee. There was so much weeds, she can't tell where she jumpin', and she jumped right into the canal. Everybody went runnin' and managed to pull her out. About a week later, she developed a bad respiratory problem, and she never, never got well. She ended up on an oxygen tank. At that time, she was thirty-six years old.

At the same time, her mom was going through it. She had another brother who was going through it. She had a brother who had died. Every one of them had blotches on their skin. Every one of them had nasty coughs. Every one of them had respiratory problems. Every one of them worked in the fields. Four of them. That whole family wiped out. Bam, bam, bam, they died right behind each other.

That's when people started saying there had to be chemicals in the water.

As far back as 1974, we talk among ourselves because we knew that when we go home at night there was something going on with our bodies. When we come to work the next morning, we'd tell each other about the toothache we had that was so bad, how our eyes was burnin' so bad, that our skin was burnin' so bad. We talk about our headaches or that we was coughin' all night long.

In the fields, if you go to talkin' about you got sick because of the pesticides, there was a hush mouth, because if you didn't keep your mouth closed, they would retaliate against you. They would tell you, "Well, you don't come back." And then you wouldn't have a job, so you had to take a lot of stuff. You wasn't dumb. You knew chemicals was being used in the field and they was against the body.

If you go right today to a farmworker's house that worked twenty to thirty years ago, they got a spit bucket by their bed. All night long till now, they spit all night. And it's no cold. It's just something in the throat—something that grinds in the throat.

Back in the '70s, the kids would be with us in the fields when the crop dusters would come over. A plane would drop pesticides on top of us. Rain it down. Some days you could look up and see them laughing. You get so mad. They took it to be funny because some of us be runnin'. I don't know what we be thinkin' about because there ain't nowhere to run. We'd fall on the ground and cover up our heads with our clothes and stuff. Some of us looking like people from Saudi Arabia with all these wraps all over us.

I remember one time, two of my childrens at the same time had nosebleeds. I didn't know what to do about the nosebleed. It would have been too weird to take a child to the hospital for something as simple as a nosebleed.

We felt it was because of the chemicals. We used to get home and we used to curse, "If that goddam crop duster weren't comin' over all day long, my baby's nose wouldn't be bleeding."

Working as a Child

I was six years old when I started workin'. While the women worked, I babysat their children in the car. And then when there wasn't any babies to be babysat, I carried the baskets that the pickins went in.

Tomato baskets, bean baskets. We had some we called the Croker sacks. I carried them to the workers at the age of six. And I started pickin' beans and potatoes at the age of six.

For the babysitting, I worked from seven thirty in the morning until six in the afternoon. And for the bean carrying, from seven thirty in the morning until seven in the afternoon if you still had daylight. From there, I would set up in the grader and grade the tomatoes, potatoes, and beans. We would grade until eleven at night. And get up in the morning again.

I started school the next year at the age of seven. I would go to school from eight in the morning until three in the afternoon, change clothes, and then we would go to the fields to pick beans till you can't see. We called it dark thirty. That's what we called it. We worked until dark thirty.

So you didn't have time, if you was in school, you didn't have time for any studying at all. That is why most of the farmworkers' childrens don't have good grades in school—because they go to work, and when they come home, they go to bed. And the next morning is school. From school to work, work to bed. So you don't have time to study.

And then if your mother wasn't educated, she couldn't help you. So that was a lot of problem for farmworker children. Their mother couldn't read, couldn't write.

My mom wasn't into education, but she tried. From the first grade to about the fifth grade, she really tried. But after the fifth grade, you could consider yourself as an adult because you're going to work those fields. I mean, education, once you make it to fifth grade, education is no longer important in your house because you're big enough then to do the hard labor work like your mom does.

I went all the way to junior high school. It was a struggle, though. With my mom traveling the season, we would leave probably two or three days after school was out in June. We would go into Maryland, where we would work in the watermelons, beans, cucumbers, and tomatoes.

Once that season finished there, we would go up into Pennsylvania, and once that season finished there, we would go up into the Hudson valley of New York. We would start back in October or November.

Sometimes the season could get as long as December because we'd travel on into Canada to gather the Christmas trees.

We would go to school up there, but a lot of migrant children loses it because their education was more advanced in the North than in Florida. So you don't want to go to school up there because you called dummies. It's just like you don't know nothin'. It's like when you go to school there, the books they read, you haven't gotten to those books in Florida. The math that they does, you haven't gotten to it. It's like the teacher is teaching a foreign language when you're sitting there, so a lot of us don't want to go to school up there.

As far as the teachers and the environment, it's beautiful, but the education is like a song you never heard. You're just sitting in class all day lost. So the kids make a lot of jokes with you, and you're already labeled as being a migrant worker. Now you're labeled as being a Florida dummy, so you lose it. And you become so withdrawn. A little child with so much weight on your shoulder. You're beat down.

We didn't have the big highways back then. It could take two weeks to get up north. We traveled in the back of bean trucks. Three trucks. One for the men. One for the womens and childrens. One for our luggage. And when we passed through towns, people would say, "Here come the tramp trucks." That's what they called us. Tramps.

Other times, they called us *maggots* instead of migrant workers.

Sometimes one of the trucks would break down. We always had a mechanic with us. So everybody get out, we build a big campfire on the side of the road and wait until the mechanic fix the truck.

In our family there was fourteen of us travelin' together—my mama, her three sisters, her three brothers, my grandmother, and a total of six children. I was the oldest child. I had a brother a year younger than me, and I had a baby sister. My baby sister, she always had to be in the fields with us. There was no babysitters back in those days, unless there was somebody in the camp.

My granny traveled with us. My granny would leave the field early and make sure dinner was done, because sometimes we didn't get out of the field until dark, dark, dark. So when we got home, my granny would have supper ready, and we always sat on the floor or on the beds or wherever and we would eat.

The childrens always slept on the floor, but the adults had army cots, and they filled the mattresses with hay.

I hear people talkin' about strangers today. How they tell their childrens about strangers. Back then, we was also taught about strangers. It was a no-no to leave your baby or your little child with somebody that you didn't know because it was a mixture of peoples. It wasn't peoples traveling up north with you from your community. When you travelin' in that migrant stream, you have people travelin' from Apopka, from Belle Glade, from Fort Lauderdale, from Fort Pierce and all down South Florida. So it was people you didn't even know, you never seen before, would be travelin' with you.

Labor Camps

We lived in labor camps, always down by the river near swamps. About forty to fifty miles from town and five miles from the nearest house. All our labor camps were far back in the woods. Sometimes we had to take chickens out of the coops at night, and we had to sleep in there. In the morning before we went to work, we had to catch those chickens and put them back in the coop for the daytime.

I slept in horse stables, where they take the horses out of the barn at night and we slept there. They get some hay, and I don't know where they get the material from, but they stuff hay into this big long thing like a pillow and that's what we slept on.

The women slept in the bottom of the barn and the men slept where they kept the hay, which we called the bullpen because all the men was up there.

They separate the men and women in the camp. The reason for that is there was limited space. The father would have to go off to the quarters with the men to give you more space in your room.

When a boy got to fifteen, he got to go with the men. Until then, he got to be with Mom. And it was just above the moms. They had a little ladder. They would come down into the stable and the mom would be right there.

But it was sad because a lot of children got to see things you never thought your child would see. I mean men having sex with other men up in the top there.

If the parent was a single mom on the camp, had no family but had her children, then the crew leader thought that had to be his woman even though he was married. He was having sex with all of the single moms.

So you a little girl, you get a chance to see all of that. I mean nothing was hid from the children back in those days. A little girl five, six years, she knows all about sex. She could tell you all about sex; she had even experienced having sex. I had a lot of little playmates, and my granny didn't want me around them because they had been indulged in sex and they was about five, six years old. So it was rough. It was really rough for a young girl.

Crew Leaders

The crew leader was the person that consider hisself to be the boss— not the company boss, but the boss of the peoples. Most farms don't hire workers directly. They hire a crew leader, who recruit people to go on the seasons. That keep the farm owner's hands clean. They say, "I didn't know."

I don't think crew leaders were licensed through the state of Florida, but there was something you had to do through the state of Florida to maintain your documents to be able to recruit people to travel up north. A lot of stuff that happenin', the state of Florida didn't know about it. There was no trackin' system as to where each person was going. Once you go to the employment office and you get your documents, nobody would know what state, or when he goin' to be in what state. So the crew leaders could get away with a lot of stuff.

The growers are white. The crew leaders are black. They mostly hire a crew leader who was really nasty, a crew leader that people feared. He could do anything he wanted to them, say anything he wanted to them, and they just squirm like a little worm and keep working.

It has been known for crew leaders and their henchmens to kill farm-workin' people. For instance, if you in a camp and you get sick or the weather get bad and you refuse to go to work that morning, we have came home from work and didn't see Mr. Paul any more. "Where is Mr. Paul?" Nobody know. Later, it was found out that they had killed Mr. Paul on the camp and they had buried his body on the premises of the camp. But the camp owners, they never knew because we come back to Florida and the talk get out. And peoples knew that the people was buried. They did the talkin', and they never reported it because they were scared that the crew leader and their henchmen would kill them, too.

We were little childrens, and we'd hear a lot of the talkin' and we'd know a lot of what was going on, but we wouldn't talk about it until we came back to Florida.

I remember in 1956, there was a guy that came on our labor camp. You wake up, there was always going to be a stranger, because people get lost and they come to the camps. When I say they get lost, they run away from whatever they running away from and they end up on this labor camp. And there was always, every morning, there was someone new on the labor camp.

And this guy, we called him DeeDee but his name was Samuel. Mr. Samuel showed up one morning, and Mr. Samuel couldn't believe that people lived the way they lived because he was some big professor at some college up north and he just couldn't believe it. He liked to drank, and that's how you hooked to most labor camps. Most migrants are hooked because of their drinkin', their drug use, and all of that.

They can't afford it, so the crew leader makes sure he keeps it. And as you work and you drinkin', your money is took. It automatically taken out of what you make.

So Mr. Samuel was there. Mr. Samuel couldn't see eye to eye to that, and he started raving about how they was cheating their people, how they was takin' the people's money. And one day, he disappeared.

Me and my brother and some other kids always be sayin', "Oh, oh, oh, you won't see Mr. Samuel in the morning." We saw it happen to people when they get the big mouth. They get beat up so bad, and we think the crew leader took them down the road and got rid of them. But a lot of times, they'd be right on that camp buried. We don't actually see them burying the people, but we knew because we seen it before.

So Mr. Samuel disappeared, and me and my brother used to go down the dirt road and dig to try and see if we could dig up Mr. Samuel. We see a fresh hole or rut in the road, and we want to dig up Mr. Samuel. We could never find him. But because of that, my family was told that there would not be a second season for us. We couldn't come back.

Packing Corn

Let me tell you a story about my mama. My mama was a celery cutter in Belle Glade, where I was born. When the celery season finished, we would go to Georgia to live with my grandmother during the summer months. But this particular summer, my mama said, no, she's not going to Georgia. She gonna follow the corn season. My mama followed the corn season to Apopka. That's how we settled here.

Back in those days, they were paying 6¢ per crate of corn. My mama got at this machine and started packin'. My mama couldn't even pack one hundred boxes of corn per day. From six in the morning, we would leave our house until seven in the afternoon, and my mama couldn't make $6.

It was production work. You want to get there as early as you could. You would sleep there if you could because your income is based on the amount you put out. It wasn't by the hour. If you didn't work, you didn't make it.

When I was ten, eleven, twelve, I was just as tall as I am now, so the boss's wife told my mama, "You got that big girl out there playing in the fields, put her on the back of the machines and let her pack."

I gets on the machine. The first day I packed one hundred boxes. No women could pack that kind of corn. The next day I packed, and on and on. And it got to where I could pack six to seven hundred boxes like it was nothin'. And my mama, she caught the devil packin' one hundred boxes.

She left the celery season because me and her could make more money in the corn season. And that was sad. You're a big grown woman with three children at the time following the season where you could make $6 a day, and your rent got to come out of that, which was $25 a week, and she got to feed three children and herself.

But then I started working and boost that $6 up.

The Muck

I remember when they burned off the swampland to make the muck farms. They would drain off all the water, burn down all the trees, and the workers—the farmworkers—would go out there and pick up those hot logs. They'd be burnin' when we picked them up. We throw them on this truck that would haul them to a pile and dump them.

Some people had gloves, and some of us didn't. Sometimes the people couldn't go to work the next day, their hands were swolled up so bad from cleaning off the mucklands. This was in 1963, 1964, 1965.

I was thirteen, and I was picking up the hot burning logs for the new farmland.

Field Work

I started having babies in 1967, and I was still traveling the season. In 1972, I had my sixth child, and I went on the season. When I came back, I said, "Well, it seemed like the same old ball from my grandmama to my mama, from my mama to her children, and from me to my children." In 1972, I said, "This is it."

So I didn't travel the season any more. I just continue to work here in Apopka during the corn season, carrot season, relish season, and doing what we call leaf—meaning the lettuce, the endive.

In the migrant stream, we worked seven days a week. When we was stable here in Apopka, you had 12 noon on Saturday until 7 a.m. Monday off.

Some people bend over all day. I don't know how they did it; I had to crawl on my knees all day to cut. That's why I'm having so much knee problems. You crawl on your knees from seven thirty in the morning. You didn't have a lunch break. If you got up to go get yourself some boxes, which you put your vegetables in, you'd take out your sandwich, and as you're walking back to work, you're eating. By the time you got back to where you left off, you drop down on your knees and you start back to work.

Sometimes the temperature be one hundred degrees out there in the fields, and we out there working, crawling on our knees. The ground would be so hot, that right here on our knees would be no skin. You would come home and you would use all kinds of stuff on your knees so you could sleep at night. You couldn't get off to sleep until one or two o'clock and you get back up and be in the field by five in the morning.

I was a big-mouth person. There was times things would happen to people in the fields, I would get raving upset and make all kinds of noise. The crew leader would go back and tell the owner, and the owner would come by and tell me I'm makin' trouble, and if I continue to make trouble, they won't be able to use me anymore. So I had to keep my mouth closed and work no matter what the conditions was.

A lot of times the field was full of snakes or rats. You're workin' and a rat run up your pants leg. You're workin', this big snake would come from under the vegetables, strikin' at you. It was just miserable. I just felt that it was something the crew leader or the grower could have did to protect us better.

Then it would be thunder and lightning. The sharpest lightning you ever want to see, and you could not go in the van. You had to continue to work. There was peoples getting struck by lightning, knocked to their knees. If we had on rain gear, the lightning would hit the back of your raincoat and bust the raincoat down your back and you got a bad burn on your body.

If you say, "Well, I can't go back to work because of being burned," the crew leader would get so mad. He would tell the grower, then the grower would tell you, "We don't have a way to take you home, so you lie in the van until the crew finish at five o'clock."

If you cuttin' the vegetables with an old hickory butcher knife and you get cut, then you got to stay there and bleed until the grower comes back in the field. The grower would come like every three hours. He be in the field at 8 a.m. At twelve, the grower come back because he want to make sure not anybody stoppin' for a lunch. On some farms, people were trained when twelve come, they go to the bus and take lunch. At other farms, the grower would automatically come to the farm at twelve and just ride or sit to make sure you workin'.

Five o'clock, the grower would come to make sure the vegetables are cut. If the order is not complete, you're going to work beyond five. You got to stay there until the order is completed. And I'm not talking about five hundred boxes, I'm talking about over ten thousand boxes. Sometimes over twenty thousand boxes a day a crew would have to cut.

I worked on a crew with twenty-five people. Twenty thousand, twenty-five thousand, thirty thousand, whatever that order is, it have to be completed. I was the highest in the cutters of the cabbage and the romaine and the chicory. I could max out at five hundred boxes per day.

There was people working in the fields that was sixty-five years of age, and those peoples was broke completely down. Those people had severe arthritis where they couldn't hold a knife to cut the vegetables, and they was given a job to pick up the crates and took the crates in the field. Their knees were so knotted from the arthritis they was given light duty jobs to do by the crew leader.

Indebted

Farmworker peoples have a tendency to stray off from their families. That's when they become vulnerable to a crew leader. He can do you any kind of way.

Maybe you got mad with your family, and you stray off. Once you stray off, whether you was a principal or a teacher or a professor, once you stray off, you are considered just another migrant worker. You connect with a camp, and they don't have respect for you. It's like they owns you. It becomes like a slave camp.

See, once you on those labor camps, you get indebted. You can't ever pay out, because you got to buy all your wine, all your liquor, all your cigarettes and your food. They never give you cash money. They claim you have used all that money for the week for eating and drinking. So a migrant worker, the average migrant worker, they smoke, they drink, they indebted to the crew leader because he sell all the wine, all the cigarettes, all the sandwiches, whatever. So you never see any money.

Those are the peoples they recruit. Why should they recruit a person who is educated and smart and know the law? They gonna always recruit people who smoke, drink, and don't know the law so they can do you any kind of way.

They don't want smart people, but they wind up with educated people. My grandmother called them educated fools. They have the knowledge, but they are a fool because they become an alcoholic, and they wander off and wind up on a migrant camp.

And when they got drunk and tell you, "Oh, I taught school in Tupelo, Mississippi," and you pick up the phone and call that school where they said they taught, sure enough, it's true. But they become an alcoholic. Alcohol follow an alcoholic follow alcohol, and that alcohol take you a long way from home. They end up all over the United States because of their drinking.

There were times after I became an adult and I got grown with all of my kids, there was times right here in Apopka we went and stole people right off the camps.

We worked alongside peoples who come here from faraway—Idaho, Mississippi—and we hear their sad stories. We told them, "If you're sincere about leavin', we'll help you."

Myself and a friend of mine, we used to go out on the camp at night. We would cut the wires and get the persons that wanted to leave.

See, what the crew leader does is the crew leader goes to the owner that owns the farm and tells them that they need to put up the fence to keep outsiders out. They have a legit story to get the fence put in, and once the farmer put the fence in, then the crew leaders control it. The owner's big house may be thirty miles from the farm so he can't see, he don't know what's going on. The crew leader controls all of that. So they put up a fence to keep the workers in. But myself and a friend, we steal them out at night.

We brang them to my house or a friend's house, and somebody would put them up. We started talkin' and tellin' them, "You don't have to take this crap. You can go and find yourself a job." And they would go to the nurseries and they would find a job. We taught them how they could reconnect with their families. A lot of them went back to their families.

Women in the Field

It was mainly women in the fields. The men only load the vegetables. The women had to do all of the cuttin'. Very seldom you would see a man cuttin' vegetables. Men thought they were too macho to cut vegetables. They want to show their muscles and throw the crates on the truck. They pack, too, because the boxes were heavy. But as for getting down there and crawling, only one crew I worked on had three men.

A lot of people used to say, "Why do women wear all of them clothes during the summer months?" We had to wear a dress so that way we could hold the dress around us when we go pee-pee and nobody could see your butt. And there was other women would gather around when you squatted down to pee, and they would hold their skirts to make a bathroom.

We had some unruly men who said, "I see it! I see it!" But they didn't have nothin' on me because I would take me a cucumber to the field and I hold the cucumber down there. If the men say they see it, I hold the cucumber. They didn't have nothin' on me. You ain't goin' to let the boys outdo you. I was the clown in the field. Still is the clown.

But if you had to do number two, you had to wait until you got home, because I wasn't going to hold my skirt out for you.

There was another thing about farmworking women that I noticed. We used to talk among ourselves in the fields. There was many women who never knew they were pregnant because we would see our period the whole nine months. If we suspect we was pregnant, we'd go one time to the community clinic, but we wouldn't go no more because we were too afraid to miss a day from work. No prenatal care.

When you pregnant, you worked the whole nine months. You better, if you want to live. I've seen woman give birth in the fields, but most times you know about what time, and you stay home. Like me, for instance. I remember one morning, I was going to get on the work truck and I said, "Oh, oh, oh," and my water was breaking. So I had to go back in the house and call the paramedics and go to the emergency room to have my baby.

But a lot of farmworker women, they get in the fields, and what we have to do, when that time comes, we make them lay down and the baby is delivered by some person in the field that knows what they're doin'. And those that didn't know what they were doin', they would just pull the baby out and lay the baby on the stomach. The crew leader would call the main office, and the main office would send out paramedics and get the lady out of the field.

I remember once, my aunt, my mama's younger sister. She got in labor and nobody in the field knew what to do. The baby didn't come all the way out because it was born breech. So they laid her in the van. She had to lay in the van until they knocked off from work. She started having it at one in the afternoon, and she had to lay in the van until five with that baby's little feet hangin' out.

When the crew leader brought her home, he didn't say anything. He just dropped her off home, and she went into the house. I happened to be coming to visit her, and I see her walkin' funny, and I say, "What happened to you?" And I see the little baby feet dangling.

I called the paramedics. But by then, the baby was already choked to death. She ended up losing that baby. Those are things that happened.

Sometimes, if you travel the seasons, when you're traveling in the North, the hospitals are so far away, you don't have a clue as to how to get to the hospitals. Most women that goes on the season, they lose the first baby or they're going to lose a baby because they don't know the town. Even the crew leader don't know the town. Most towns are like maybe thirty miles from the camp or more, so by the time you get to the emergency room, that's it.

Back in the '60s, I began noticing that a lot of our newborn baby girls were seeing periods. A lot of women talk about that from Apopka. They would see it like a normal period, three days or so, and it would disappear. If you didn't take them to the doctor, it lasted up until their time really started. I know women who didn't worry about it because it was such a tiny amount of blood and it was three days.

I talked with a lady the other day, and she and her husband are scared to death because their daughter has been having her period since newborn, and now their little girl is seven years old. They afraid that the little girl could get pregnant at seven. You find women talk about it all the time. It's so secretive if a black women's child is going through those changes. They don't want nobody to see my girl's having her period at eight years old because it going to get out in the community, then some bum might try her and she end up with a baby at seven or eight years old. It's scary. So most women who work on the farms keep their stuff secret.

Singing

To keep us motivated and to keep us high-spirited in the fields no matter what the workin' conditions was, we used to sing. There was always someone in the field who could really sing. One woman might start off—nine out of ten she gonna be a Christian woman—and she'd start off singing. "Hmmmm, run and don't look back, run and don't look back." And other workers would repeat, "You better run and don't look back. You better run and don't look back."

Another song we sing is, "Get right church, and let's go home." It was one of our slave songs, and they had a lot of powerful meaning. "Get right church, and let's go home. I'm goin' home on the morning train." Meaning: We fittin' to run away. The train is our runaway. So we tellin' the slaves to get ready so we can run away. We don't have time for what's been going on in the labor camp, so we gonna run away. All the workers, they know those slave songs. We were taught those songs when we were a little girl.

Another one is, "I'm gonna lay down my burden, down by the riverside. Down by the riverside. Ain't gonna study war no more." Meaning, You better meet me down by the riverside because I'm layin' all my burdens down. I have gotten tired of pickin' all these tomatoes, ain't gettin' paid, so I'm laying all this burden down. I'm gonna be down by the riverside because we plannin' to book up.

Those songs were codes. A lot of white people had no clue because we would not tell them. If we really didn't want our master to hear, we'd hum a tune the others knew the words to. "Hmmmmm . . . hmmmm . . . hmmmm . . ." And then somebody would sing, "Before it's too late." That mean, "Get up here before it's too late, because we goin'."

We sing these songs every day if we see our boss comin' because he gonna retaliate against us. If we angry with him and we want to get a point across, we sing in a nasty way, "He will look like a monkey when he get home." We pickin' at our boss. He don't know what we talkin' about. He think we talkin' about one another, so he laughin' along with us. But he the one that gonna look like a monkey when he get home because he been treating us so bad. We can laugh about it now, but back then, we was dead serious.

Today, people say, "Look, you got better workin' conditions. You got drinkin' water, you got restrooms in the field." But the pay increase is worse. I know a lot of people don't want to compare the '50s with today, but in the '50s, '60s, '70s, and half of the '80s, you didn't have to pay child care. You could take your childrens in the field with you. Now child care for a baby is from $100 to $150 per week.

Now they have rules and regulations. You have restrooms in the fields, and you have drinking water in the fields, but it costs you. I cut a box of chicory for 25¢. And right now, that's all they're paying. They're still paying 25¢.

And corn. When I started packin' corn, I was a little girl. Corn at that time was 6¢ per box. I'll be sixty-one years old the sixteenth of this month. Corn started at 6¢ a box, and you're only getting 20¢ a box right now. You're talking about fifty something years later.

Sickness

In 1972, I decided I wasn't going to travel again. We were working for a farm here in Apopka. We were just getting over the spring crop and coming into summer. It was a hot, hot summer that year.

I had all six of my children in the field with me, and that day when we left the field, I noticed my baby Biddy wasn't looking good. She was three years old. Her complexion was real dark. Real, real dark. When I got her home, I give her a shower. I cooked, and I sent everybody to the dinner table. Everybody was eating but her; she was leaning to the left, leaning, leaning.

I went there and pushed her up. I said, "What happened to you? Sit up and eat."

She would sit up and she would start leaning again. I couldn't figure that out. So that night, at midnight, it didn't get any better. She wouldn't go to sleep. She was whining, whining. So I take her to Orlando Regional Medical Center. When I got there with her, they treated her for meningitis. I brought her back home.

The next night I had to go back. They said it wasn't meningitis. They couldn't find out what was wrong. They sent me back home. This kept getting worse, worse.

So the next night I took her to Florida Hospital on Rollins Street. They checked her out, and that's when they determined she was having a stroke. She had a stroke at the age of three, which left her crippled in the left hand. She limps when she walks on her left leg. Her eyesight was real bad. It left her with epilepsy. She had what they call grand mal seizures until she became an adult.

I think she was thirty-four years old when they came out with the new brain surgery. They go in and put something in the brain stem and run it under the skin to her heart. We looked at that surgery, and I didn't like it. We decided to do another surgery. They did that surgery in Shands Hospital, and she broke the seizures. She don't have the seizures no more. But she can't use her left hand. She limps on her left leg. Now she wearing a brace.

After she had the seizure, it was hard. It was really, really, really hard. Having six kids, being a young mom, I didn't know what to do. They put her on the CMS [Children's Medical Services] clinic, and with me having appointments after appointments with her and me trying to work those fields, it was rough. If I missed one appointment, the state would give me such a hard time. And it was really, really, really rough.

I have a brother who was born without the bones in the bottom part of his arms. He can take his hand and roll it up to his elbow. It looks like a shrimp. A big shrimp. Both his hands.

My mama was a young woman that never did any type of drugs. My mama don't even like anything for headaches. No kind of medication. They want to believe that my brother was deformed because my mama was pregnant with him and my mama used to bend over and cut for hours and hours and he didn't have a good chance of development when he was in the womb.

We worked in the cauliflower for years with headaches, never knowing what was causing the headaches. The cauliflower was grown on a plastic sheet. Under that plastic sheet was tubes, and years later we found it was gas. That why our head hurt us so bad. You could smell gas all day. But we thinking it was the machine. But it was that methyl bromide or something that they was using.[1] We used to have to go in the fields and run those tubes, not knowing it was gas. Stick the tubes in the plant and then put the plastic sheet on them; and when the cauliflower started developing, we had to take the tubes out and pull the sheet. So you were in the fields eight to nine hours a day working with all of that pesticide in the fields.[2]

We eat food right in the field without washin' it. That was a strike against us because nobody told us we couldn't just split a head of lettuce open and eat the heart out of it without washin' it. We did it all the time. People just shuck an ear of corn and just chew it.

Some of us didn't take our childrens to the field, so the question is, "How would the child be sick?" What they failed to understand, they had the cutest little canisters and baskets where they had the pesticide in the plastic bags. We bring that home. That basket, my baby socks goin' in there. My flour goin' in there, my meal going in there, my sugar.

I can't afford to go downtown to Jordan Marsh and buy a canister set. So that pretty thing be on my counter with my flour and my sugar.

For years we did that. We just come home and wash it out with soap and water. We didn't know about pesticide, but the residue was still in there.

We washed all the family's clothes together. We didn't say, "Oh, I'll take all of these pesticide clothes . . ." Uh uh. We washed our white clothes with everybody's whites. Our colored clothes with everybody's colors.

Sometimes we come home soaking wet, drenched in pesticide, and we pick up our kids and hug them. Their lips be right up against our shoulder, and they would get blisters in their mouth. We thought it was thrash and we'd mop out their mouth with bluing [fabric whitener].

I've been a diabetic since 1974. I have congestive heart failure and lupus. Sometimes my joints just lock up. But I didn't qualify for any medical benefits until 2007, so all that time, I gotta find someone else who qualifies, and they share some of their medications with me.

Current Day

There's not a night I go to bed that I don't remember, and I know the womens is still out there workin' in the fields. Right now, my heart goes out to Latino women when I see them living on the labor camps because I know what they goin' through. My story is nothin' compared to what the Latino women are going through today. So I can laugh at my story.

The reason is that the Latino women are undocumented, coming across the border. Once you get in America and you start working as a migrant worker, that crew leader know you undocumented and he gonna handle you any way he want to. Where are you gonna run? *Where are you gonna run?*

As for me, there was a time I left the camp walking. I grabbed my six children and I left the camp walking because I refuse to take crap. But where they gonna go? I know the United States. I learned about the United States in school. I can read maps. But where she gonna go? I know what their daughters are goin' through. Yes, it's crucial for them. It's crucial.

I know a camp right today where undocumented farmworkin' women live, and they are threatened with prostitution. You getting raped every night. You gotta have sex against your will every night. They got to do it because you don't have nothin' if the border patrolmen know you are here. You are goin' back to Mexico, and even worse there.

How you doin' better than you did in the '50s? In the '50s, if a man treat you like that, you got a kickback because you got your family with you. But they don't have nobody with them. So it is sad.

Our government just passed a law in Washington to use a chemical on tomatoes that is worse than DDT. *Worse*. I worked in DDT, but this chemical what they using now is worse than DDT.

I have a brother born with no bones in his arms, but the Latino people have children born without eyesight, some with no arms or legs, some with other severe problems.

If you see some of the Latino children in South Florida, their moms workin' in those tomato fields, oh my God—you wouldn't have enough cheekbones to hold your tears.

5

"God Made Up for My Lost Children"

Earma Peterson

Earma Peterson offered me my pick of one of her great-grandchildren if I promised not to bring him or her back. The comment brought a hearty laugh from her forty-year-old son sitting shirtless across the room connected to some sort of breathing machine. He was recovering from a surgery that removed a mass from his liver. A few years earlier, he had double bypass surgery, and a few years before that, triple bypass surgery.

We were sitting in Earma's living room and people of all ages kept entering from the front door, back door, the kitchen, a bedroom, another bedroom. I finally asked how many people lived there (no definitive answer) and how many family members she had (no definitive answer). So Earma, her son, and an adult daughter who happened to wander in at that time began naming Earma's children, grandchildren, great-grandchildren, and great-great-grandchildren while I kept the tally. We did not count spouses. With much laughter and going back to delete named great-grandchildren from one family to add them to another, we reached a total of one hundred.

Before long, I had an invitation to Thanksgiving breakfast, when the family all gathers. Apparently this meal is more important to Earma's family than Thanksgiving dinner itself.

I asked about the picturesque grassy hill just on the other side of her fenced backyard. That brought another laugh. It was a landfill that had only recently been covered over. For years they had put up with the sound of dump trucks, the smell of garbage, and the circling and pooping and squawking of gulls. The dump had been approved years after Earma moved into her house.

At the end of the interview, Earma said to me, "People ask why I have so many answered prayers. I tells 'em it's because I listen to God." With piercing, penetrating eyes directed on mine, she went on to say that she believes I, too, must listen to God since I am writing these stories.

With a backward glance at the covered landfill, at the house that holds so many and so much, I climbed into my Dodge Avenger, parked in Earma's dirt driveway, and drove away, humbled by her words.

I was born in Crescent City, Florida, in 1930. July 21. My mother and father separated when I was four and a half years old. She married again. My father moved here to Apopka and I stayed with him on Boy Scout Road on premises in an orange grove. My daddy worked for a man that had a house out there. Our boss man was up on Apopka Boulevard going into Winter Garden, and we was back up in the orange grove in the house. As I grew up, there was nothing here but woods. All this here was an orange grove.

My father worked grubbin' up roots out of the ground, or they be plantin' orange trees for somebody, cleaning up a field to put orange trees in. He did a lot of things like that.

He was paid $3 per week. Back then, you get five pounds of flour or five pounds of sugar for 5¢. You got meal for 5¢ and 10¢. That could last you a week or more. That gives you a chance to get something else.

We didn't have to buy no canned goods like pork and beans and stuff like that. My father raised his food, and we had to can it. In the summertime when there wasn't no work done, we fished. My father would take that fish and salt it down for the winter. Now you don't need to can no food no more, but I do it sometimes because I like preserves.

I went to school in Orlando until I was in sixth grade. I walked about three miles every day to school from Wescott Road down to Eighteenth Street. Every day, three miles to the school and three back home. I finished elementary school, ninth grade.

Earma Peterson. Photo by Gaye Kozanli.

When I was eleven and a half years old, I started menstruating. I got real scared and so did my daddy. He contacted my grandmother, who contacted my mom, and I went to live with her.

My mom had a fifth-grade education. She didn't have many opportunities, and her second husband said she couldn't go places or do things. I wanted more for myself. I wanted to go to high school, but this was before integration, so my choices were limited. There was a boarding school in Eatonville—Hungerford High School.[1] My mom couldn't afford for me to live on campus, so from Monday morning to Friday night I stayed with my grandparents, who lived at 8890 Cornstalk Avenue in Winter Park. I walked about four miles every day to attend classes and be with the children on campus.

When I was twelve and a half years old, my first job was in the fernery. I worked out in the John Mathis Fernery in the summer. After then, I started working on the farm at night cuttin' celery. We had to pack the celery. We had to pack escarole. My mom would come with me and stay out there on the job.

I was eighteen or nineteen when my first baby was born. I didn't marry. I didn't want to marry. My mama didn't force me to marry. She say, "Well, you don't have to if you don't want to." So I didn't.

As time went on, and when I got about twenty-one or twenty-two years old, I married a guy from Alabama and went there to pick cotton. I left him in Alabama because I couldn't stand that cotton. They paid you by the pound, and cotton didn't weigh nothin'. You could pick all day and not get a pound!

I came back and went to work on a farm pullin' corn. They had something they called a mule train. It was some kind of tractor, but they called it the mule train. When you pull the corn, you had to throw it on up, and you had to keep up with it just like you was keeping up with somebody riding a bike and you was running behind it and you would be runnin', too. You didn't just sit back and not worry. If you want to get your rows, you be runnin'.

The first time I was working behind that mule train, I carried two rows. People from Pahokee down by the Everglades was pullin' corn, too, and this one particular lady showed me how to do four row. When I get down the other end, she said I wouldn't have but two to come back on. Depending on your age and how well you work, you got more rows.

Working on the Muck

I cut beets, chicory, celery, cabbages, lettuce. And when we was working, they had the aeroplane. The aeroplane would be dishin' out that pesticide on the plants. They wouldn't tell you they was comin', and you'd get sprinkled on. If you wasn't covered up good, you'd get it all in your face and all on your skin. But I learned. When I went out there, I took my hat and put my gloves on. I had a big hat that fit over my face and over my shoulders to keep the pesticides from messing up my face.

One thing about me, I always looked out for my face. A lot of people don't look out for their face. I don't want it spotted up or look like it been burned in the fire. And that's what that pesticide would do for you. You ever seen a person had smallpox? How smallpox do your face? Sort of like measles. And that's what the pesticide would do your face if you scratched it. It was bad if you really let it touch your skin.

When you's workin' on that muck, you get up four in the morning—I still wakes up four every morning. I walked nearly three miles to catch the truck to go to work. That was a long ways to walk to go to work. That truck, that man in that truck, he don't care how far you stay. That's his pickin' up point right there.

Twelve or thirteen workers be on the truck depending on how many people work with that particular contractor. At first, you just jump on the truck and sit with your legs hangin' down. Well, they stopped that, and the man had to put sides up. Then you had to get up there and get in the truck and you had your own bucket or bench to sit on. You set up on that until you get to the job. You take your bucket off, set your lunch on it, and when you ready to go back from work, you put it back up on the truck. They didn't furnish nothin' for you.

Workin' on the farm was a tiresome job. But along then, I didn't get that tired. I was young. Walkin'. Runnin'. Now I can't run. I don't do no walkin' too much cuz it hurts my knees.

I was workin' with Linda's grandfather. He was a hard man to work with. We had like a sixty-acre ground. A row might be a thousand feet.

If you hoeing, if you pullin' corn, if you cuttin' escarole, if you cuttin' celery, that's how long those rows was. And by noon, you had to have a row out because we on the other end. Comin' back down this end, by the time you gettin' ready to go home, you have that one out. You have two rows going down and two rows coming back. If you was thinnin' corn, cuttin' celery, cuttin' escarole, whatever you were doin', you had to be a good worker. Then we had to watch out for the aeroplane.

One thing I did was cut beets. When you pullin' beets, you have to pull 'em in a way that they don't bleed. If you pull 'em and they get scarred or holes or something in them, that drains the blood out of them. You can't be throwin' them around in a hurry. You got to know what you doin'. If you don't, you bruise it and it bleed.

When you pull up a radish by the top, you just clip it like that and you let it drop in the basket till you get it full up. The radish is red, but that don't bleed like the beet do.

I picked beans. Different types of beans. They're more easy, because you can get a basket full of them quick if you knows how to do it. When you reach up there and you see them hanging down, you take it like that and you throw them in there like that until you get to the top. You have to have thirty-two pounds in a bean crate.

The crate be on the ground when you pickin' beans. If you on the first row, two rows, or three rows, you can set the crate on the side where the truck come down. But if you in the center, you got to carry that thirty-two pound crate to the truck.

The saddest thing I ever seen on the farm is a guy was plowing on the muck with the tractor. That part of the land had never been worked on, and when he went out there, the tractor and him both went down in the ground. The muck just give way. They had to come all the way from Orlando to get the ambulance because they didn't have no paramedics. When they finally got him out of there, they take him over to Orlando Regional Medical Center. ORMC was the only hospital—nearly twenty-five miles from the farm. They needed more hospitals. They needed more doctors.

So I be on the job by seven, get out at five in the evening, be home by about six thirty to seven in the evening.

Then I have to see about my children. My mama had them all day. I had to feed them and give them a bath because they were my children. She said if she was dead, I'd have to do it, then do it now while she's livin'. So that's what I had to do.

Back then, we didn't have bathrooms in the house. We had our restroom on the outside of the house. We used to call it the lavatory or the toilet. It was like an outhouse. They had that on the outside, but you could take a bath on the inside of the house with the tub in there. We didn't have no 'lectric stove. We had a wood stove. A big wood stove. Mama would have water inside when we come in from work, and we could take a bath and go to bed.

We had to heat the water on the stove and put the water in the tub. To empty it, we take the tub up, carry it to the door. It was heavy. I could pick up a half-full tub; sometimes I picked up a whole tub of water if I'm washing, depending if it's a number two tub and not a number three. If I picked up a number three, Mama have a fit. But number one and number two, she would say okay. Number one is smaller than a number two, and a number two is smaller than a number three. Then you had the long one that look like a bathtub. That's what we called a number four. It was made out of tin.

We had tubs to wash clothes and stuff in. It wasn't like it is now. You had to pump your water. You didn't have a spigot. You had to pump it, and you had to carry it. We had to carry water from here to the corner of that road down there, maybe a quarter mile or so. Sometimes we carried water further than that just to drink. We had to wash, we carried that water a long distance. Sometimes we come to the lake. There was a lake here, and there was a lake on the other side. We washed our clothes at the lake. We had a big red wagon. Put all the clothes in a wagon and pull them all back home and put them on the line. We don't have to do that now. We've got washing machines. The water flow in, and sometimes you're too lazy to do that.

We had a rough time washing dishes. Now we put them in a dishwasher and come about our business, and come back and don't feel like takin' 'em out.

I met my second husband in a bar in 1954. Married him in 1968. His mama died when he was two years old, and his brothers and sisters raised him. One of his brothers lived in Pittsburgh, and he wanted to go and live there. He didn't know how to drive, but I did. I had even purchased a car, so we moved to Pittsburgh.

He want to stay up there, but I said life was too fast for the children. I told him, "I'm goin' back to Florida and raise up my children. You don't have to come if you don't want." So I left him up there in Pittsburgh.

Children

I stayed with my mama until my fourth baby was born, then I got me a house of my own. I raised ten children. I had sixteen, I raised ten. One of them died about two years ago, so I got nine. Seven boys and two girls.

I miscarried six children at two and three months along. I didn't know in the beginning what was happening until I got on further in years. One of my girlfriends, every time she was workin', she was losing every child. Come to find out, the doctor sayin' that's what was wrong. Workin' out there on that farm.

When I was pregnant, I worked up until a week before, or three or four days. I had three of my children at home. They come quick and I thought they were goin' to come.

I miscarried six children, but I gained them back. My children, grand-children, great-grandchildren, and great-great-grandchildren number over one hundred.

None of my children worked on the farm unless they have a holiday. I took them out to pick beans or something like that. In the '70s, I would take my boys to the orange groves and to the fields, let them work. Let them experience what work was about. When they workin' in the orange groves, I wanted them to learn how heavy those sacks was, how much was in a bin, how long it takes to fill a bin and earn $6.

I told them be settin' a goal for what you want to earn in a day. Maybe $100 a day for oranges, workin' all day, early to late. I taught them to work to get what you want. You can't sit around.

My father used to say that when you work for something, it's yours.

You work with your own hands, you earned it. You use your own brain, it's yours. If you didn't work for it, it's not yours.

So when my children worked, that money was theirs. I said, "You take that and buy what you need—paper, pencils, shoes, whatever." I wouldn't take it for one reason—that make him not want to work.

Current Day

Today, I'm a diabetic. Lots of farmworkers is diabetic. I have poor circulation, and sometimes I don't think clearly. My back and my knees bother me quite a lot, and I have arthritis. There's different types of arthritis. I think mine from inhaling pesticides. This leg, I have an artificial plate in it. This one, I got a pin in it. Trying to keep my legs. Tryin' to keep them from cuttin' them off.

My son had triple bypass surgery, then, about two years later, double bypass surgery. About five weeks ago, they pull a mass off his liver. He's got a breathing machine. He's only forty years old. They don't give a reason for these medical problems, but I think it has something to do with what I was workin' at when I was carrying him.

I got my house in '83. I put in for it in '78. It took a long time to get it. I had to push 'em at the last minute. I had to push 'em to go ahead on and get it and finish it. I think it had something to do with the bidding.

After I moved in, they put a sewage treatment plant just over the hill. You've got the big old tanks right there. If we had known they were going to put that up there, we wouldn't let them do it. They did us the same way about that medical waste incinerator over there—they burn up plastics that shoots poisonous gas into the air, and they might be burning body parts, too, we're not sure.[2] Then they want to put another one over there on Keene Road.

They did these things without us knowing. They said they had put it in the paper, but we didn't see it. We didn't hear it on the news or nothin' about what they was going to do. They just went ahead and did it. Once they get started, couldn't nobody stop 'em.

Then they want to put that compact in for them diesels coming in with their garbage. They want to build a big old thing like a garage where they could back that in, but people want it over on Hog Head

Road and SR 441. They was talkin' about they gonna put it down there, and I don't know where this Caucasian man come from, but he said no because that's his daddy's land. He don't want nothin' out there on it. That was about a fifteen-acre ground. He wasn't going to let them put it out there. They haven't put it up yet.

Years ago, they had lights on the other side of town, but not on this side. We had to beg for them.[3] We were persistent because we knew that the money was already there.

There's a lot of things right now on my mind, but I have to wait because sometimes the words don't want to come out. But this I know—I can't go back and change what's behind me, but I can live up to what's before me. I've been blessed. I thank God each and every day for His blessings.

6

"I Might Have Been an Actress"

Louise Hamilton

Louise Hamilton arrived for her interview with a plastic grocery bag bulging with pills and a ream of medical reports dating back decades. Since I was willing to listen, she was eager to talk. She told me about drinking filthy keg water in the fields and developing stomach cancer; she told me about climbing up and down ladders for years and developing arthritis; she told me it took her two weeks before she could tell her mother that she'd been raped in the field; she told me about the day in 1980 when pesticides from planes got in her eye and she went blind.

At the time, I had not yet interviewed Mary Tinsley, so I didn't understand the connection between lupus and hair loss. Louise weaves hair she purchases from a wig-making shop into the tops of panty hose to create all sorts of hairdos that are lightweight for the heat and humidity of South Florida.

These days she takes care of her great-grandson, who has ADHD and autism. She calls him her little company keeper. He is going into the fifth grade and knows computers backward and forward.

She said, "Me and him know how to 'municate. When I say, 'That's a no-no,' he say, 'Don't bother that.' And I say, 'That's right. That's a no-no.' Then we talk some."

Louise proudly held up a picture of her mother, who worked thirty-one years for one farm. She fell one day, cracked her head, and broke her tailbone. She died less than two months later, never having received insurance or retirement money.

She told me all of this with shining eyes, an occasional short laugh, and pride in her voice for the life she has lived.

I would have liked to be an actress. I would have liked to be somebody to teach kids. I would have liked to be a hairdresser. But my mama had twelve kids. She worked in the fields, so from the age of seven, I watched my five younger brothers and sisters. I never had a childhood in my life. I never even had a doll.

I cooked, washed their clothes on a rub board. I had to tote water two or three blocks from a place called Tin Pan Alley. I didn't go to school. I learned myself how to read and write.

We didn't have a father with us at the time. My mama raised us without a father cuz she said they keep givin' her babies. I didn't know where she gettin' 'em, but you know how that is. We didn't question her cuz we know not to.

My mother come home, I don't care how tired she was, she'll put somethin' to eat on when we were small. We had a kerosene stove, two burner. When I got a little older, I cooked. I been cookin' since I was seven.

When I turned sixteen, Mama said I had to go out to work with her. When Mama got sick, me and my oldest brother, named Donnie Hamilton, worked. I go with him, and I got the hang of it. You betta get the hang of it. If you don't make no money, you in trouble. I got a lot of whoopin'.

We picked green beans by the hamper. They was only payin' 55¢ per hamper. I watchin' my brother. My brother picked twenty-seven hampers. I barely could do five to six hampers. Then we get to the far end, they have fried fish for you to eat. You had to buy your sandwich and your soda. He charged you a whole dollar for two things. If you eat up all your money, you got a good whoopin' when you get home. Sometimes, I'd take $3 home.

You had to work really hard to make some money. You had to pick the right kind of beans. You couldn't pick all of them. If they find little ones in the basket, they pull 'em out. You had to learn to stack the

Louise Hamilton. Photo by Gaye Kozanli.

basket to make it fill quick, so when they come and hit it down, if it fell over, you gotta put in more. Then you got to tote the baskets over four rows to the truck row. It was really, really hard.

I worked with watermelons in Apopka. I was on the grader. I could thump 'em and know when they ripe and when they ain't. If it sounds really light, it's not fully ready. But if it sound in between heavy it could be too ripe when it sounds BOOM BOOM. If it's [high-pitched sound] thunk, thunk, it's not ready. Some watermelon you see in the store, they green all over, but if you got yellow on the bottom, it more might to be ready. So we had to learn all that.

A perfect-size cucumber like you make salad is ten inches. If you get them longer than that, they've got big seeds in them, and they don't taste good. You can get them too small, and they ain't ready. You got to get them at least ten inches, and they got to be a certain size around. They give you a measuring thing. Once you measure them one time, you could figure about all day what you gotta get.

We had a ring to do that with the lemons, too. They didn't want the lemons too small. The great big ones overripe, overbig, overlarge. They didn't take those because they not good to sell. They cut the price, the boss man say. He say, "Y'all can't get those cuz it'll mess up my crop this year."

So we try to get him the perfect stuff. He'd give everybody a ring, and he'd let you use it for a while, then he'd come back and get them. After, he'd check his stuff and see how you doin'. He'd say, "Good, good," and we'd know we had a good boss man. So we'd try to make him happy by how we worked. That way, he wouldn't lay you off and not pick you up and get somebody else.

See, if you didn't work right, they wouldn't come by your house and get you no more. They'd say, "We don't need you today. We got some-body else in your place." And that's hurtful. Especially when you think you got a job. So when you get a job, you works real perfect, got to do it just the way he wanted it so that way you keep a job. I don't care how tired you got. You gotta pay your bills.

I'd be on the bus at five in the morning. They had benches with can-vas depending on how cold it is. They called it the ring line. That's what they called it. The ring line. Other boss man drive the truck to take you to work. If you ain't on time, he cut you $1. You ain't gettin' but $12.50

a day, and they take 50¢ of that for Social Security. The boss man on the truck, he'd be gettin' paid by the head for bringin' people. They pay him for his gas and pay him by the head. That's how he made money, the man who take you to work.

I was always there on Monday because if you weren't there on Monday, he didn't want you there on Tuesday. Cuz he feel like you've been off since Friday, now you ought to come on Monday. So I made sure I didn't miss on Monday.

You could fool around all day in the field if you wanted, but if you can't pick three to four bin, he not gonna say, "Well, you'll pick up a little bit next week. Maybe you'll do a little better next week when you get the hang of it." You better get the hang of it the first week, or you wouldn't have a second week.

And then the airplane come and spray—you didn't get out of the way, cuz if you go runnin' out the way, the boss man say, "Where is she going?" So we mostly wore a wide hat if you could and long-sleeve shirts. Once they spray on you and you out there in the fields, that really eat you up. It was like bugs and acid eatin' you up. I got marks all over my legs. They were bad on my arms. The skin clean off of me. But you had to work. I would use a lot of cocoa butter.

I got raped in the field once. See, you didn't have bathrooms. You have to go out in the bushes behind somethin', so that's what happened to me. I was out in the bushes and I got raped. I couldn't tell my mama for two weeks, and then she beat me for not tellin' her. I wasn't going to tell because it was my boss man, and if I tell, then my mama don't have no job.

You had to drink water. He'd bring us kegs of water, set it on the field, on the end, on a block. Some people go up there and stick their hand in it and get the ice out. And you got to drink it like that. I had so much germs and stuff in my stomach, I had cancer. It had been in there for years. I carried it around and carried it around and carried it around, and I was scared. I knew my stomach was hurtin' me all the time, but, you know, when you thirsty, you drink a lot of filth.

In 1989, they had to go in and take a lot of my insides out—one of my ovaries and half of my stomach. They didn't get it all, so it bounced back after all those years. Then they had to go down my throat in 2009. I was scared they might cut the wrong thing.

When I got about eighteen, I went and got me a job at the nursery totin' roots from plowed up ground. Cuttin' the tape off. I know how to make seven trees into one tree. You had to bud a tree and make one tree and build seven different things out of one tree. You had to learn all that. Then they had a little tape on the bottom. Some of it's gettin' a little yellow, and it's ready for you to take the razor blade. You gotta get on your knees. You can't cut the tree. You can't cut away the bud. You gotta cut it in a certain place or the boss man fire ya. I did that for over a year.

Then I started workin' on tomatoes. You had to take the string and tie up tomatoes to keep them from baggin' and saggin'. They have to be tied straight so they can grow straight so when they ready to be picked, they won't pull them out of the ground. I did that for nine years.

They didn't turn Social Security in, and I didn't find out until I was grown. Nine long years. They paid $12.50 per day, and they'd take out 50¢. Every day. They put it in the books for Social Security. Then when the time come and I got grown and in my sixties, I went for my Social Security. The people told me, "You only got thirty-four credits. You need some more credits because the nine years you worked down there, they didn't turn nothin' in off that."

They gone and died now. Nothin' you can do about it. So I left that alone.

After that, I went up the road, worked in Apopka, 150 miles away. For three years I stayed on the camp Sunday night through Friday. Met the boss lady. She got thick hair, now it got a little gray, but she was so nice. Every Friday, three o'clock, she would bring our check. Every Friday, three o'clock.

We did bell pepper, corn, pickin' in the fields, packin' in the packin' house. Every Friday we made a little more. If we borrowed something, she wouldn't take it out. She didn't like to learn about it, because she'd say, "That'll cut you short." Which was nice.

I stayed out from the graveyard. You didn't have to pay no rent because you was workin' for them. It was nice because you had your own little room, and you could close your door. They had a big 'frigerator. They had a bathroom and a shower right there in another building.

I'd leave on Friday after work and drive one hundred fifty miles home. I had two ladies waiting for me to do their hair: $6.50 a head. I also did perms in my house making extra little change, but then I wasn't able to do it when my eyes got bad. People don't want you burnin' their head up. I would leave on Sunday and go back up so I could be to work on Monday.

I just had three children, three girls. That was three too many. My sister takin' care of my kids. She didn't have none, but sister dead now because she had sickle cell. She died at age forty-three.

Later on, I worked under Elijah James, and he would let my girls work on Saturday. I would let them keep that for their allowance money. Cuz I didn't want them growin' up and takin' money from mens. I made every one of them finish school. I didn't want them to have to go out and work in the field like I did. After high school, they joined the service. My daughter Mary stayed in the service eight years. She met her husband there. They been married twenty-six years now.

My mama worked thirty-one years for one farm and she fell and cracked her head and broke her tailbone. She had sugar, and she didn't want to take her shots no more. She died in less than two months. She never did get her money for herself gettin' hurt, and she never did get no money from the thirty-one years. Never got her retirement. Never got her insurance policy that she wasn't using. She wouldn't go to the doctor. No matter how sick she got. She would always say, "I've got to go to work this morning cuz Mr. Wayne is 'pending on me."

After Mama passed, her baby boy David got killed in prison. I'm glad it didn't happen when she was alive. He was doin' things he got no business doin', runnin' his mouth, tryin' to fight the police. They kept puttin' him in the hole. When he got out, he took to smokin' rocks and didn't pay the man. The man hit him hard in the head. They took him to the hospital, but then they said he was all right and they take him back to prison. He died in prison with a cracked skull. The police told me to look and see if it's my brother. He had blood comin' out his nose. They say he been bleedin' like that for a couple days.

He wouldn't be fightin' like that when Mama alive. She would get the battle stick. She'd put a whoopin' on you. She didn't spare you no rods.

Oh, God, I could tell you so much. I don't forget none of it. I went through a lot in life with workin'.

In Apopka, we did corn, string beans, bell peppers. Bell peppers— you gotta get the right size. You can't pick 'em too small. They give us a thing like a ring to kind of show the size of what you supposed to pick. Because if you do it too small, when it go to the packin' house, they throws all that away, and that takes a lot of work out the fields. We wouldn't have work as long if we picked the stuff before it ready.

I liked workin' by the day because then you could work steady. She didn't want you to kill yourself. She just want you to not play around, just keep up and do your work right, make sure the baskets are set up right. Make sure the peppers set in there, not thrown in there, you know, get bruised all up. We had us a little bucket. It's easy to put it in the basket. We set it over a slider.

My favorite part of workin' on the farms was pickin' oranges. I like to pick oranges because I made the most money pickin' oranges. The first two-three days, you are some kind of sore. Every muscle in you sore cuz you not used to toting all that stuff and grabbin' all day.

First you have to go into the middle of the tree and get 'em all. Then you climb all the way up the ladder and pick on your way down or you could string yourself. If you don't put that strap on front and you slip through the ladder, you will get strangled. I slipped through the ladder once. It hurted my knee and it hurted my shoulder. Stay out a couple weeks, you gotta go back to work. But then I learnt.

When you fill your sack, you go and dump it, then come back up your ladder where you stopped. It was a big sack, but you've got to learn how to fold it down to your size. It was a kind of hook, you'd bring it up and hook up and make you half of a sack and then it don't be so heavy to try to drag and tote. So the boss man showed me how to do all that. I got a little hang of it. Every now and then, I'd drop a few. I tried not to drop none.

At first, I was pickin' four bins. They payin' us $4.80 for a great big old bin full of oranges, and I realized I had to take two rows to make some progress. First I had buckets, but that didn't work because you can't tote a bucket goin' up the tree and carry your own little ladder. I had to tote my own ladder. Some people, they worked with their husbands, and their husbands tote the ladder.

The boss man found out the wooden ladder was too heavy for me. I was only ninety-five pounds, so he got me an aluminum ladder. I went and carried two rows. I wind up pickin' seven to eight bins a day. And then Friday they called me, and when I got my check, it was $107. I was really happy. I was *really* happy about that. I made good money then.

The straps on the sacks could cut into your shoulder, so you could make your own pad at home with overalls and stuff, make it thicker, that way it don't cut you skin. That's why you see most people with big needles makin' pads and things when they work in the fields. Even knee pads, cuz if you got out on the ground without knee pads, them stickers gonna get you. They gonna stick all in your knees so you can't walk, and the next day you cut your knee open tryin' to get it out.

It's dangerous work in the fields. Dangerous work. Especially fruit. Fruit is more dangerous than string beans. Fruit is more dangerous than bell peppers cuz they don't have stickers. Anything with stickers and thongs like them lemons, oh God. That's why they pay so much a bin for lemons: $15. Because you got a bin, you done work. It takes a whole lot of lemons to make a bin. Them things have thongs, you gonna wear three to four shirts, sometimes they stick in that. And then you gotta have gloves.

It's hot. You betta go out early in the morning. *Early* in the morning.

I worked and I worked, and then in the summertime, when there was no fruit to pick, they would let us clean around the trees. You know, pull grass around them and do little stuff. It would give us something to do so it wouldn't be so long between the seasons.

I never drawed unemployment in my life. A lot of people draw unemployment. I don't know what that is.

I like pickin' oranges and I like budding them trees. Take a lemon tree, I could make it into an orange tree. I could take an orange tree and make it into any kind of tree that a bud go in. Grapefruit. Lemon. Orange. Have all that on one tree. But you're gonna have to take some sticks and help brace that tree cuz them big old grapefruits, they would bend them pretty good. Then if you got the lemons on there, and your oranges on there, you've got to keep it propped like I was telling you how we did the tomatoes with the string, puttin' it on the stick. That help make it grow straight. You could look down the row and it looked so nice and everything when they grow up. You could tell what's ready, what wasn't ready. All you have to do is reach and get it. You didn't have to look all on the bushes to get snakebit.

I worked too fast to have problems with snakes. They'd get out my way. Only time a snake gonna bite you is if you scare him or you too close on him. They'll strike you. But if he see you first, he gonna start movin'. So out in the field, you know, I used to be up in the tree pickin' oranges, and I watched out in the ditch, and they had these big old snakes called gopher snakes. They break the other snakes' backs. They just wrap around 'em and break their backs. They were real big black snakes—sometimes nine feet long. Big and fat. They put a lot of them in the fields to keep the other snakes out while people work, the kind whatta bite you. And they'd be down there, laying up in the ditches.

They don't hardly bite people. They will scare you enough. I will always look up in my tree before I go in it. Even if you have to pull the bushes back and look all around in there, you'd better, because the fields was by the canals, you know. They spray the fields and they plow the fields and they come through there with that big old thing with sprayers and they keepin' them wet, keepin' the bugs away. Snakes love wetness, and if they didn't put them gopher snakes in there, a lot of people would have got bit with snakes.

One day I was workin' real hard. One was up in the tree, and that tree was loaded with good fruit, and I was tryin' to get it done so I could make me one more bin before four thirty. I'm over halfway finished with the tree, and when I moved my ladder, something said, "Look up in there." I looked up in there, and my heart went to fluttering. Where I done picked, that snake went round that side. Out of my way. Cuz he said, "That lady gonna throw me in her bag if I don't move."

It scared me so bad I left the whole tree. I just had but two more stands with the ladder, and I said, "I can't do it no more today."

The boss man come and said, "Okay, Louise, I imagine." That's all he said. He knew I don't leave none on the ground, and I know how to pick my trees.

He sent one of the guys up there to make that snake get down and go in the ditch. Oh, he was so big and long. I don't know how I didn't reach him and grab him, but as I picked, he would move around out of my way.

When I see the bus comin', I know it's four thirty. They want you to be out of the field by five o'clock cuz the truck driver bringin' you home goin' to his home to eat. That about the size of it. He ain't messin' around with time when it's supper.

One day in 1980, I was out hoeing in the field, and the planes started comin' and sprayin'. I went blind in the field with the poison. They worked on my eyes and worked on 'em and worked on 'em, and in 1991 they couldn't save them. They put more lens in, and they still flame up every so often. Any time they feel like it, they do it. I got appointment go back to see me every year. Next month, the fifteenth, at ten fifteen in the morning so they can take these out and put barrels in and make them go for another year. But you know, I thank God I can see, because one time I couldn't even see. It's bad when you can't see.

I stay on meds for arthritis because I had to tote ladders and heavy stuff all my life. I think that's what caused my joints, knees, and stuff like that. Sometime they get to where I can't walk. They had to put steroids in my foots. Dr. Gray at the health clinic told me it's from standing on hard things, sharp stuff and having heavy stuff pressing. You get where your foots, you can't walk on them, and your ankles, they put steroids in them and needles.

It's hard work, workin' in the fields. But that's the only work you could do if you didn't have an education. So you go out there and you work hard, but you wouldn't expect to go blind and get cancer and arthritis and all that.

7 "Learning the Hard Way"

Mary Ann Robinson

In 1962, when Mary Ann Robinson was twenty-four years old, she had saved enough money to buy a piece of land on a quiet country road in South Apopka. At that time, you could use the land as collateral to have a house built. She's been living in the same house ever since, having paid off the mortgage after fifteen years.

Besides working on the muck, Mary Ann worked in the nurseries and ferneries in South Apopka, where she learned about plants. Over the years, she has turned her front yard, side yard, and backyard into a little oasis. She has pineapple, pecan, peach, palm, orange, and lime trees; peppers, grapes, figs, watermelon, and a blackberry bush; honeysuckle, philodendron, ferns, roses, and cacti; mustard, turnips, onions, and collard greens—to name a few.

In the meantime, a sewage treatment plant went in across the street. She says, "It's been a problem because of the odor." At the time, Mary Ann was working full-time and caring for her mother, who had Alzheimer's disease. "I don't know whether we mighta coulda went to meetings to prevent it," she laments, "but at that time I had to take her to day care where they see about her durin' the day, and I would come and pick her up in the afternoon. I was so caught up with her and tryin' to work that I didn't . . ." She sighs and cannot finish her sentence.

Mary Ann Robinson. Photo by Gaye Kozanli.

Once an establishment with negative environmental impact makes a foothold in an area, others will soon follow. Before too long, a practice area for firemen went in next door to Mary Ann. Down the road are a firing range for policemen and several landfills, and not too far away is a medical waste incinerator.[1] Including hospitals, clinics, nursing homes, laboratories, funeral homes, pharmacies, and dentists', veterinarians', and physicians' offices, there are approximately thirty-eight thousand facilities in Florida that generate biomedical waste.[2] In the entire United States, there are fifty-seven active biomedical disposal facilities and only one in Florida that is "open use," meaning it is available for use by any entity licensed to handle medical waste. It is the one in South Apopka.[3]

In this once-rural area, the traffic to just one landfill can be as many as ninety trucks a day.[4]

Mary Ann says, "I tell you, they done put so much down in here. We've been goin' to meetings and trying to kick against things. If you don't have a lot of money and they put all this stuff around you, you can't just up and move. So it's just a bad situation."

My mom, that's all she did was work out on the muck. She come from Alabama. She moved to Apopka figuring she could have a better life here because in Alabama she was just doin' housework. Workin' in people's houses. Her daddy, my grandfather, was here in Florida. He had a sister here, and that's why he came to Florida. I don't know if you ever heard the sayin' "Money grows on trees in Florida." My grandfather and his sister were sayin' about people makin' a good livin' pickin' oranges. My mom never did pick no oranges, but she did get a job out on the muck.

I was thirteen years old when we moved here. The way I started workin' out there, like when school was out, like the holidays, she would take me out there with her. I hoed escarole and chicory. You know when they be small, you hoe 'em and then, when they get ready to harvest, I would cut them with a medium-sized knife. You cut 'em and clean the bottom off and you packs 'em in boxes. I never did get hurt. I was taught good how to use the knife. I bent over all day. It was rough. The rows are so long.

I started workin' full-time on the muck when I was about sixteen because I dropped out of school. I stopped in the ninth grade. I just wasn't interested in school like I shoulda been. When I quit school, Mama made me go to work on the muck, and that's what motivated me back to school. You know how sometimes you get caught up with the wrong crowd and you feel like you don't need this because they don't have this. I'm talkin' about like education. But once I came out of school, I wasn't able to run the streets or whatever because Mama made me go to the muck with her. Then I seen what a blessin' that it was for me to be in school.

Sometimes your parents can talk to you all they want to talk to you, but you do not pay them no attention. You have to learn the hard way. And that's what I did, because once I left school, she didn't make it easy for me no kinda way. She didn't let me idle around and do nothin'. She said, "Hey, you made your bed, you do whatever you need to do to make a livin'."

I got experience of what that muck really was like and how I didn't want to spend the rest of my life out there. It wasn't easy. That was hard work. Bendin' your back, breakin' your back from seven to five. Sometimes we'd have about thirty minutes' lunch. We didn't have no breaks. Thirty minutes' lunch and that was it. Back then it was outside bathrooms. It was just terrible. But that's all we knew.

I didn't work on the muck as long as some of 'em did, maybe about five or six years. But anyway, I don't wish that I hadn't had that experience because I think that experience made me what I am today. The muck made me want to better myself. It made me want to get better education because I see what the peoples and myself went through when we was out there on the muck. I'm more dependable. It motivated me to want to have a home of my own and a nice car to ride in, and I knew that in order for me to get that, I would have to get a better job to do what I needed to do in life.

The muck and the nurseries was the only thing 'round in here where you could get jobs unlessen you was highly educated. So that's where we made our livin'—out there on the muck.

I had to get up early in the morning, maybe leave home around six a.m. in order to get to work early. But it was okay, because that's all we knew at the time. I used to cut chicory and escarole, and we were just getting $5 a day, $25 a week. That was back in the late '50s and '60s. They had something they called a mule train, and they would pay you by the boxes of corn that you would pack out there on the muck. We worked over and over doing the same thing. They didn't have no unions or nothin' like that out there at that time.

We'd be workin' and the planes, they would come over and spray us, but at that time, we didn't know it was affectin' us no kinda way. We just gotta hold our head down until that dew and stuff passed by and went on the way. We didn't stop workin'. We just knew that they sprayed, and you could feel the dew fallin' when they come over.

At lunchtime, we would make a fire and heat our food in order for us to eat something warm. The wind would blow seeds over by the canal and greens would grow. We would carry some of those greens home and cook 'em for food. We ate a lot of stuff that was raised out on the muck. We didn't know about the chemicals.

You know, when I was workin' out there, the only thing I can remember was blacks workin' out there. It wasn't no Puerto Ricans or Mexicans here at that time. I don't even remember no whites out there.

I think I was nineteen when I got my GED. I heard Disney was hirin'. That was back in '72, right when it was opening. I had finished school and everything. I went there to get a better job. So I stayed out there twenty-one years. I worked in the laundry. I was a lead in the laundry. I have lots of certificates for workin' at Disney for so long. It was eye-opening to me because I started out with $2.05 an hour. I left in 1994 and worked my way up to $13. I stayed long enough to retire—I retired early to take care of my mother.

When I went to Disney, I knew about hard work because of the muck. I knew how to work, and I really thank my mom for instillin' in me about work. I wasn't afraid of work. So with the muck, I think that helped me become what I am today because she instilled work in me from a young age of what I had to do to accomplish what I wanted in life.

I did a square in the memorial quilt [chapter 13] for my mom. The significance of the picture I made of her, I remember her with pants up under her dress, so that's the way I made the picture from my remembrance. Gettin' up every morning, puttin' the pants on because see that muck would bite you when it would get dry; but bein' a woman, back then didn't too many women wore just pants. They wore dresses, but to keep the muck from bitin' 'em, they would put the pants on underneath the dresses. The straw hat is on top of her head in that picture. So I just made it the way that she dressed when she went to work.

My mom died of Alzheimer's when she was eighty-one, but she started having health problems when she was fifty. She had heart problems. She had sugar. They wanted to amputate her little toe, but we wouldn't let them because her hip was deteriorated too bad. I really believe those chemicals can get in your brain and stuff and can cause all kinds of problems.

I'm on the board with the Farmworker Association now, plus I goes to meetings tryin' to prevent a lot of stuff from happenin' that did happen in the past.

I believe that regardless of what situation a person is in, whether it's the muck or where, if you really put your mind to it, you still can accomplish what you need to do in life. Everything's hard till you learn to do it.

8

"I Wish They'd Bring the Farms Back"

Betty Lou Woods

Betty Lou Woods leaned over the interview table with a sparkle in her eyes and an easy laugh in her voice. She told me her stories with two or three repetitions for clarification. And every so often, she reached into her large black purse for a tissue to gag up phlegm.

She knows how to bag carrots, and now I do, too, after her detailed step-by-step instructions that start in the field and end with a million bags on a pallet.

"I won a trophy once," she said, laughing and gagging. "They called me Miss Bright Eyes, and I won a trophy." At the end of one year, it seems, the grower had a big picnic and asked everybody to bring a homemade dessert, not only for consumption but for a contest as well. Betty Lou, of course, used carrots as her main ingredient—grated carrots, whipped cream, walnuts, and fruit cocktail. The memory has brought Betty pride for at least twenty years.

Betty Lou sings in her church, but not—unlike her twin sister, Betty Doe—on YouTube. Betty Lou wasn't satisfied until I Googled her sister on my Smartphone. We watched the video together. Betty laughed into a tissue, pointed at her sister's antics, and together we shared a moment of camaraderie.[1]

Betty passed away in spring 2013.

Betty Lou Woods. Photo by Gaye Kozanli.

I wish the farms didn't get destroyed. I wish they would bring them back so the young people could get off the street and go to work every day, have something to do. A lot of generations hang on the street corner and sell drugs. But if they had fast money, that'd be great. Some people at the farms pay you every day. I'm telling you, that was a good help in my day. People need it now; they bein' laid off from jobs. That would help our community if they brought the farms back.

True, you hurt later. You've got aches and pains on your legs and on your back workin' on the farm. But I thank God cuz it was a lot of help to the family. Farmwork helped us to live, to be independent. I knew my mama to make $200, $400 a week, but they didn't take out Social Security. My mama didn't put her money in the bank. She kept her money home in a secret place.

My mama had sixteen living children. She lost two twins. I'm a twin. I got a identical twin sister, Betty Jean Doe. I'm Betty Lou and my twin sister Betty Jean. We had twin brothers born before me and my sister that died. We all got the same mama and daddy. Now all of them dead except eight of us. Half dead and half living. Four brothers and four sisters.

Our original home was in Jacksonville, Florida. When I was five years old, we lived down south in Belle Glade and Pahokee, another town called Bean City. We were down that end towards Miami. I remember my brother shook the trees, and we would pick up the limes and put them in the bucket.

I remember pickin' beans down in Belle Glade. I had about three classmates die. A lot of families used to take their children out of school and bring them to the fields workin' to help make fast money. If they not in school so many days, the truant officer's gonna come and check the fields. When the truant officer comin', my mama say, "Lay down." But other mothers tell their childrens to run.

The bean field, the string beans, is next to the sugarcane patch. They run into the sugarcane field, and the stalks is tall. Taller than you and I. They about twelve feet tall, and by you runnin' in the cane, you can't see nothin'. And on the other side of the field, they burnin'. They used to burn the cane before they cut it. If you in the center of the field, you don't know where you at. Like the cornfield. That corn and sugarcane is real thick. It's so thick you can't even see through it. You can't see nothin', and nobody know you in there. Take a helicopter to find you!

At the end of day, when the truant officer leave, the mama say, "Y'all come out, come out, come out." The tractor makin' all that noise, the trucks makin' all that noise, so the parents can't hear the child. They don't know where the child is. Later, people who owned the fields or one of the workers would find them. They lost their lives. They suffocated from the smoke and got burned. Not ashes burned, not crispy.

In the field they have a canal. A lot of the classmates jump in the canal runnin' from the truant officer. They be runnin' and jumpin' in and get drownded. It not that wide, but if you can't swim, muck is soft, you can get stuck in the muck and that child gonna drown. I seen one child drown. They tried to save him when he went under the water. They called somebody who could swim. Before the truant officer or somebody get to them, he's gone, because the muck—the black muck—be in the bottom of the canal and they sink down.

My goal was to try to finish school, but I never made it because of workin'. My grade level was third or fourth grade. When I was in my forties, I took a test. They say I was the sixth grade level. I started to take classes for my GED, but I never did get it. I can read and write, though.

After Belle Glade, my mama started travelin' from state to state wherever they had farmwork. New York. Pennsylvania. Maryland. Virginia. New Jersey.

Up north, we lived in camps. I remember a camp in Virginia. The contractor be so mean to the people. He brought the men and women up north to work, and he worked them so hard. He *work* 'em. They have to pay for eatin'. They borrow money to eat. The contractor would sell a loaf of bread for $2 at the time when bread was nothin' but a quarter or 50¢. A can of Spam lunchmeat, he charge $3 when the store sell it for 25¢ or 50¢.

If you workin' for a contractor, the head man over the whole camp, they got a big old kitchen, and that contractor and his wife, they run the kitchen. The people come there to eat, they going to charge you $5 for that plate. If you eat lunch, that's $5. If you eat supper, that's $5. That's how they used to do people. When you get your check—your cash money, they didn't have no checks—you might make $200 to $300 that week, but you wind up with $50. So when that person workin', they take all the funds from 'em. Take all the checks, the cash money. Some people workin' for nothin'.

My mama don't play that. My mama scraped. My mama kept us, she fed us, she gave us supper. But some people had to depend on this contractor.

I saw them beat people like slaves. Some people try to escape. I saw once, in Toano, Virginia, near Norfolk. We stayed out on a camp near the farm, and the man beat this man cuz he didn't want to get up and go to work. He beat him with a big stick. A broom handle. Make him work that day.

You couldn't call the police. You out on that farm. At the time they have no phones on the camp. If anybody had a phone, it'd be the contractor, and they'd never let you use it, so they do the people like that.

My mama worked on farms in Apopka back in 1956, '57. She got to where she loved it, so she stayed. She bought a home here in 1963. She died of a heart attack in 1989 when she was seventy-seven.

I've been married twice. My first one, I was seventeen. I met him on the farm in Delray Beach, Florida, and we were workin' in the packin' house. He was from Mississippi. He's the father of my children. I ain't got none from my second husband. We lived in what they called camps, but they were like apartments. They were nice. Everybody had their own apartment with their children. Sometimes we'd be in a house. Sometimes it'd be a little apartment. The contractor, the person that you workin' for, made sure you had a place to live. The light bill and everything was free. Just had to get up in the mornin', the parents go to work and the children go to school. After school, you go to the field or your mama come and get you.

I visited my mama in Apopka a lot, and I began to love it here, too, so I moved here when I was twenty-three. Got divorced not long after. Only married to him eight and a half years. He was a cheater, running around.

I liked working in the packin' house on one of the farms on Lake Apopka in Zellwood. At least you be out of the sun. Some day they have you work in the field half a day and then go to the packin' house. But other farms were different.

They had a carrot house. The truck come out of the field with the carrots and back into the grader. Once the carrots fall into the grader, they got a great big deep tub washin' them and they comes up on the belt for you all clean. Then, as the carrots roll down the belt, you got a group of people pull the rotten ones, take out the ones with the spot on it, throw it away, and by the time it gets to me, the one that baggin', them carrots already clean. All I got to do is bag.

My section of people, we did one-pound bags. Other lines did two-pound bags, three-pound bags, or five-pound bags. So each belt had a different size bag of carrots. Two people would face each other across a table. Me on this side and you on that side. About twelve people on each side. Standing up. We had to stand all day long.

I have a whole sleeve of bags, and they hooked onto the table in front of me. Like when you go to Winn-Dixie, you see they got the bags hooked on the circle. Maybe I had two hundred bags on a sleeve, maybe five hundred. The carrots come down the belt, and I pick up a handful and lay them on the scale. The scale was long, shaped like a carrot. It was a balancing-type scale. I pull out a bag, tip the scale, and dump the carrots into the bag. I flip the bag, twist it, and tie it. They had an automatic machine to seal 'em. Then I throw it down the chute.

When the machine started goin', no stoppin'. As the machine go around, the carrots go around. They never fall on the floor. They go 'round and 'round until that belt empty. As you pick 'em up, they baggin' them. As fast as you puttin' on, they takin' 'em out.

Sometimes carrots got stuck, and the scale got locked up. The man got to fix it.

When they bag 'em, then the guys have to put 'em on the pallets, the bags just stacked. He had to put fifty pounds or something like that on a pallet. During a week's time, they probably have over a million bags of carrots.

I worked there the longest.

Workin' on the muck was more hard cuz you got to be in the field and the dirt and the dust. You have to mind what you doin'. You have maybe thirty, forty, fifty people in the field, so you got to cut so many acre. Each person got two row. People fast, they carry four row.

They kept the fields sprayed, so not too many snakes in the field. I never seen a rattlesnake, but a man got killed once. He run up on him, surprised him. You'd see little bitty small snakes. And if you comin', makin' noise, they gonna go on up the road. They goin' way up in the field, be tryin' to get out of your way.

I liked pickin' pickles. Cucumbers. They call 'em pickles when they little. I like pickin' the pickles because you work fast. Sometimes you get fifty to sixty baskets and you get more money at the end of the day.

They low to the ground. You got to put your hand in the vine, and you see 'em on the ground. You pick just a short ways down the row, and you get a bushel. They be plentiful. It don't take long to fill up a basket. Better than pickin' the cucumber. You straddle the row, and you just pick up that vine, pick that side, then this side.

I also worked in tomatoes. I picked them and packed them. Leanin' over, pickin' all day, your back gets tired. But that didn't bother us, because we had to work. You pick so many acres. As you pick the tomatoes, you put them in little wooden baskets, ⅝ baskets we called them. You put peppers in wooden baskets, too. Bell pepper, jalapeño pepper, yellow squash, eggplant go in the wooden baskets. Sometimes they give us red plastic buckets we called foot tubs. They the same size as the ⅝ baskets.

Cauliflower, cabbage, and eggplant we put in crates. An eggplant vine tall, maybe three feet tall, there'd be about thirty eggplant on one bush. They multiply. Eggplant over multiply every day.

Cuttin' cabbage was dangerous. A lot of people have cut themselves bad. I cut my thumb and a lot of things. You got a big butcher knife. About two to three inches wide and twelve inches long. The knife be sharp. And then you're going to hold the cabbage in the middle and you take the knife and cut it. And there's a certain way you got to lean that cabbage to cut it. You've got to straddle the row, walking down cutting it. When it's cut, you throw them in a pile. Then the truck come along and load them up on a big flat-back truck.

I used to carry two row. And it'd take you a whole day to pick all the way down. They had the rows so long. Whatever you did, the rows so long. We used to do five or six rows. You'd be tired at the end of the day, but that's the way we made our livin'.

If you were cuttin' corn or celery, you'd get some shade because the machine that cuttin' the celery is big. It's movin'. You had to walk behind the machine all day long. The machine for the celery made the same way as the mule train for the corn. Only thing about that, you had to walk behind and cut the celery. We had about twenty people walkin' behind cuttin' the celery. The knife that you cut the cabbage, you do the celery and throw it on the belt. Like airplane wings, you cuttin' the celery and throwin' it up on that belt and sendin' it up to the person on top that packin'.

When you packin' celery, you got to put the butt end this way and the butt end that way. Front, back, front, back. Till you fill the boxes. Thirty-two stalks to a box.

I worked seven days a week at that time.

I'm the mother of five. When I needed extra money, I would take them to the field with me on weekends or when school get out like for spring break. Give them a chance to get out so they earned money. All my children, all five of them, would come with me to work. They were about ten or twelve at the time.

I lost a son who died at thirteen. He was in sixth grade, and he was in elementary school. They were going on a field trip in a van. He was in school and they brought him to the YMCA and they were taking him swimming. He got a bug out of the water and he further got sick. And it broke him out in a rash. The next thing I know, he was bleeding out of his nose and I didn't know what happened to him. When he got sick, all I know is doctors come from all over. They come to run tests, and they say he have some sort of rare disorder, aplastic anemia. He died of that. A rare blood disease, his white blood cells in the bone deteriorated.

When my son got sick and they say he had a rare blood disease, I wondered if it could have come to him from chemicals in the fields with me. It could have affected him and I didn't know it.

He had to get a bone marrow transplant. Had to go to Seattle, Washington, to try to get some cells from my other son, who was a donor. But he didn't make it. He died in Seattle, Washington, at the age of thirteen. So workin' on the farm all that chemical and stuff. I was pregnant, too. It could have affected him down through the years and I didn't know it. It could have come from me being around chemicals and the area where we live. It was in 1979. On the weekend, he worked on the farm with me.

Another of my sons is disabled. He's in a wheelchair. Had a tragic accident in 2001. He's paralyzed from the waist down. He was driving a little Nissan, and the Lynx bus pull out in front of him, and he went through the windshield. The bus driver didn't see him. He stayed in a coma seven days. He was walkin', but he's not walkin' anymore.

I've seen tragedy in my lifetime.

I met the Farmworker Association back when it first started. I got involved. I thank God for the Farmworker Association. They are good people. They help a lot of people even though a lot of people died from chemicals from workin' in the field where they sprayed the vegetables. They got arthritis and lupus and all that stuff. I thank God that during that time, the Farmworker helped us survive. All the years the Farmworker always been a help.

They helped me paying bills, light bills down through the years. Food. Pampers for my grandchildren. Farmworkers is a good organization.

I met my second husband in 1982 in church. I was a soloist and lead singer in the choir. I love to sing. He played lead guitar. He worked at the Sentry Plant in Plymouth running a machine to make juice cans. He was a good provider. We've been together almost thirty years.

It has been a good journey for me to work in the fields. I thank God I made it. Survived. My mama taught us to work to be independent, work and take care of your children, so I always been a hard worker. I tried to be faithful.

I don't work now, because I'm disabled. I'm sixty-seven, and I thank God I'm alive. I stay home. Just me and my hu'ban'.

9 "My Daddy Went Blind in the Fields"

Robert Griffin

Mr. Griffin lives down the street from where he was born in South Apopka. As he told me about the events of his life, he pointed in one direction or another to indicate where they had occurred. His mother, his father, and his grandfather all worked on the muck. His wife worked on the muck, hoeing and doing other jobs. Her mother and grandmother worked on the muck.

Although Mr. Griffin is in his late sixties, he still directs a small crew of about twenty farmworkers in citrus groves because right now he's "only doin' somethin' to be doin' somethin' cuz it's in my blood." He says, "You don't find too many people thirty years old pickin' oranges now" because the pay "is the same as it was thirty-five to forty years ago." He predicts that in the not-too-distant future, the orange groves will be turned into backyards because of the pay, because most farmers can't afford to prune the rows properly, because of the canker disease and the greenin' disease, and because of all the storms that come through. Another problem is the "two-trailer limit." Farm-workers are paid piece work, not hourly. His crews used to pick between four to six trailer loads a day, but now they are limited to two. This drastically cuts their pay.

He and I had quite a time understanding each other—I with my Bostonian/Brooklynese accent and he with his Deep South accent. On the day I called to schedule the photograph session, he said he wouldn't be home and we should come to another address. Five times I asked him to repeat the address. Finally I understood that he would be at the junction of two roads I was familiar with. I figured it wouldn't be too hard to find—there would only be four houses, one on each corner, and I knew he had a pickup truck.

When I arrived with Gaye, my photographer, we spotted several pickups in front of one building. Four older African American men were sitting on vinyl-seated, steel-legged kitchen chairs leaning against a boarded-up building. Mr. Griffin was one of them. The beds of the pickups were filled with watermelons they were selling.

Sitting, chatting, selling, and waiting for us.

My dad was from Alabama. When he was in his twenties, he got tired of plowin' with a mule. Come twelve o'clock, the boss man give him a lunchtime. My dad tied the mule to a tree and hoboed a train down to Florida. He was stone barefooted when he got to Florida. A lot of people around here came from the same place in Alabama. Some came down here for the good of themselves and some didn't.

My father went blind thirty-five days afore I was born. He was just past thirty years old. He was spraying Paragon in orange groves. They don't put no mask over the face or nothin', and the chemical got in his eyes and took the whole pupil out. Just wasn't nothin' left to 'em. He didn't get nothin' from no insurance company or nothin'. The only kid he ever saw was my older sister. That's the only one he seen. So the rest of us, ten kids, he never seen none of us.

He went to Bethune Cookman College in Daytona and learned how to do different things, like make pocketbooks and belts and things like that. He used to drink. A white guy uptown at the liquor store told him, "You're throwing away your money drinkin'." He went home one night and got drunk and started thinkin'. He stopped just like that. His mind went straight to business.

He was blind, but he could handle it pretty good, you know. He could take money and feel it and tell you what it was. If he met you right today and hear your voice right tell your name, he'll know you ten years from today. Yes, he could. He had a sense of humor and started getting

Robert Griffin. Photo by Gaye Kozanli.

a lot of breaks with different jobs and things. He made a life pretty decent.

Childhood

I was a little boy, about seven years old, and I used to go out to the muck with 'em on the weekends and cut relish, kale, pick string beans. All that kind of stuff. I worked all day. We were havin' fun. We didn't know about how many chemicals we takin' in at that time.

When they cuttin' relish back in there, they payin' about $2 a box. We go out there and cut three to four boxes a day. Somethin' like that. And then a lady be out there with a sandwich wagon. We were young. We cut a box of relish, we go take our money, go buy a pork chop sandwich. The pork chop sandwich ran maybe about a dollar.

I learned to drive early. I started drivin' my daddy's truck in the fields when I was six or seven years old.

I was born up the road in what they called the White Quarters. Little shotgun houses there. We had the Dollar Quarters, the Graveyard Quarters, the Brown Quarters.

I could remember when we was livin' in the White Quarters. Chief of police was Mr. Bill Dunnaway. The constable Mr. Fred Reisner. They knew everybody in town. They knew everything criminal goin' on. Mr. Fred knew everybody that sold moonshine. Lot of guys sold moonshine. My daddy sold a little moonshine, too.

On Sunday mornin', Mr. Fred come around the back door. Knock, knock, knock. You doin' wrong, you give him $10 at the back door and he'd let you know when the feds comin' in. He'd tell you, "Boy, don't do nothin' this week. Them boys be here." Sunday morning, back door. Always Mr. Fred.

My daddy bought a brand-new '53 Buick. A black man have a Buick back in them days, that was real fine. I was about five years old. Knock on the door that Sunday mornin'. As Mr. Fred passes by the window, Dad say, "That's Brother Fred."

I open the door. Mr. Fred say, "Little Dude, tell Blind Dude he gettin' rich. Now we need $15 a week."

They caught a few guys sellin' moonshine. They never did catch my father. They knew there was something, but they never did catch him.

They went to court. Johnie McLeod, he was a city lawyer. He would tell them, "Blind Dude take care of family."

Mr. Fred, he was all right. He could catch 'em on the street doin' wrong. One day he was right behind me. I was with someone who stole somethin'.

He say, "Now boy, you know that nigger law stands. Don't tell me no lie. You know I can take you to jail."

I said, "Mr. Fred, please don't take me to jail." Said, "I'll come up with the money."

Fred get up and walk off. I said, "Mr. Fred, I'll tell you what. I'll give you $5 you don't take me to jail."

He stop. "You wouldn't be tryin' to be bribin' me, boy."

"No, Mr. Fred, no!"

He walked another five steps, then he stopped and said, "You know I live over there. There's a mailbox in front of my house if you want to come by."

Mr. Fred, he'd call you a nigger. He never called me that, but I seen him call guys that and slayin' names; he didn't want you to lie to him. He asked you a question, he wanted you to tell the truth. I never seen him raise his hand and hit nobody either. Never.

Mr. Fred had a little black Ford he ride around. He catch those guys shootin' dice in the street. He watch till they get all the money on the ground, then he and Mr. Clint pull up. Everybody jump up and run.

I was a little boy. I used to say, "Whose money this here?" Weren't nobody claimin' it.

Mr. Fred say, "I guess mine, me and Mr. Clint." He'd get it and put it in his pocket. "Y'all, boy, get some more money and put it down there. Me and Mr. Clint got our water bill to pay."

Water bill about $2 a month long in then.

Mr. Fred died a few years ago. He'd be ninety-seven years old. He still planted a garden. He had tape to try to keep his eyes open, man.

Black and White

My daddy 'bout got killed one night out there by the school with that same black Buick. I could 'member that like it was yesterday. That was in 1954. That was a horrible night. Man asked Daddy to bring some moonshine to 'em about two or three o'clock in the morning. When my daddy and mama got there, they kidnapped them. They stopped the car out by Dream Lake. Daddy told Mama to jump out of the car. She ran back to town. They looked for my daddy all the night. They thought he was dead. They know the car burned up there by Dream Lake. They wondered if he still in it or not. They found him the next mornin' walkin' 'tween Apopka and Plymouth. One of the guys recognized him and picked him up and brought him back.

Everybody know who did it. A white guy. But they didn't put nobody in jail for it. They squashed it. They sent 'im away. We never seen 'im from that day to this one. But they buy my daddy another new car and give him $1,000 to keep it hush-hush. That's all they did. You could tell things now you couldn't tell back in then. There was some good people and there was some bad ones. It won't never go away.

I got an old blackjack. All the police got them back in then. When you hit somebody with it, it just spring back. Someone got in a scuffle out in front of the house in the White Quarters. One of the polices dropped it and I got it. I was a little boy. I never will forget it. A little blackjack with a spring in it.

Dr. McBride, he was white. Years ago, if you got sick, he would help you. He took care of all the black children down here. You'd go out to the house at night, he'd help you . . . in the kitchen. I remember that just as good. I went plenty of times. I cut my knee one time right here in the White Quarters. I sat on his kitchen table and got stitched up.

He told me, "Boy, I see you do a little rough playing. I'll tell your daddy to stop lettin' you play in that glass out there."

My daddy built the apartments over there on Park Street. If you put up a door, he gonna feel it. If it not right, you gonna take it down and do it right. That's the way he were. Our home-house, the big brick house near the big river, it got twenty-six doors in there. The room-house got thirty-one lockin' doors. My daddy had a ball of keys.

He says, "Robert, you go and open the door."

I couldn't find the right key. He feels the keys and goes in every do'. Every one of 'em.

On the Road

In 1952, we went to New York for like a vacation. We was in town one day. My mom went in a little country store. A guy needed some 'mato pickers. He thought we were on the seasons. We weren't thinking of workin' at that time.

The guy said to my mother, "If you've got anybody that wanna come out and pick on my farm, I'll pay you $10 a head for 'em."

Me and my dad was in the car, and my dad heard. He had a good sense of hearin' and smellin' and stuff like that. He said, "We're gonna try that."

We get three guys out there from the place we were stayin' at and that was $30. We went out there, too. I think I picked about fourteen baskets 'matoes the first time bein' in a 'mato field. Real ripe 'matoes. And mother picked 'bout 170. They were payin' like 10¢ per basket. That was a lot of money along in there, man. That was a *lot* of money. Gas like about 13¢ a gallon back then.

After that, my daddy said, "I'm gonna get me a truck and start comin' up on the seasons."

In Florida, the labor board would meet him and people would apply for a job. That's how he got to be a contractor.

I went to school in New York. Ain't too many guys went to school with white people. I go up on the seasons and they treat me real nice. I had no slayin' names told me. We was in Dutch country. They came by and checked to make sure we had food to eat.

I got three whoopins when we out on the seasons. One for not workin', two for being hotheaded in school. The first one I got, my mama told me to pick seven hampers of beans every day. A hamper of beans was thirty-five pounds. I worked out throwin' stones at a groundhog in the fields and I picked five. She tied some bean vines together and tore my butt up. I was eight or nine.

From the time I was seven, I had to buy my own clothes. In summertime, I saved up $200 to $300. That was a lot of money back then. Bought two footlockers for the clothes. You get a pair of rugged jeans for $2.99. Pair of good khakis, shirt, coat. For Easter and Christmas, they buy me toys, but they would buy me two suits for Christmas, two suits for Easter. And all the other stuff, I bought. My daddy said, "I'm gonna make a man out you." During the summer when I weren't in school, I gave my mama and daddy $10 a week. That's for eatin' and board. They just tryin' to teach me how to be a man and take care of myself when I got up. Now I'm glad I did.

My dad had a good name for hisself, and everybody from Florida to North Carolina to New York and them places was calling for the blind man. You couldn't mess around with him. He was strictly business. One thing my daddy never did was sit down a week or two and wait for the crop get ripe. He leave home on time.

My dad was probably the first to buy a bus to go up the road carrying the people. He bought a brand-new '58 Ford bus. Cost $4,000. Back in the '50s and '60s they still carrying people on the back of trucks. We'd take about twenty-five head of people up there, and durin' the late '50s, '60s, we ended up workin' one hundred twenty-five head pickin' beans and tomatoes and eye potatoes in Pennsylvania. We work for Chef Boy-ardee pickin' 'matoes for the spaghetti and sauce.

Another place we take people to work is about seven miles off Lake Ontario. It get cold up there, it get *real* cold. We go up there, school get out. We take a lot of school kids up. And the parents didn't go. We bring them back in September to go to school. But along in then, you could take young children, fourteen-, fifteen-, sixteen-year-old children over there to work. But in this day right now, you couldn't do that.

School generally get out the first to third of June. We leave the day after school get out. We go up on the seasons. Sometimes we had so many people we had to take two trips. Wasn't no 95 then, all them big highways. They were goin' back roads up. You know what I mean. Wasn't no McDonald's. Had to stop, eat cold cuts the side of the road, you know how the days were. There were a few bathrooms the blacks could use. Stop and go in the woods. Only a few truck stops we stopped at to get gas where you could go in and eat. We had to go around the back.

I 'member once there was fifty-four of us. I think this was in '55, between '55 and '57. I got a good remember, I just can't place the year right now. We's going through Charleston, South Carolina, on 17. Dad told where to stop and get everyone something to eat. The lady told we couldn't stop there with the men in black. Send one of the ladies back and get the hamburgers. My mother went back down there and got fifty-four hamburgers. They were 25¢ apiece. They put 'em in a box. We got down the road, gonna eat 'em. Open 'em up. They had two slices of white bread, lot of lettuce in the middle, and the hamburger about as big as a quarter in the middle of 'em. And you couldn't give 'em back to 'em.

Just something we had to go through back in that time. Everybody wasn't like that. We met some good people on the road. We ran up on some bad people.

My mother walked the fields and did the payroll. I 'member when the labor board man came back in '58. I was pickin' beans. He told my mother and father they got to start takin' out Social Security on the people. And we had to keep that Social Security money straight. They make $100, $3 come out of there. It was all straight then. We take the Social Security money, put it in a separate place. They come along about once a month, maybe twice a month, the government people, they picks it up. We kept pretty straight books. Never had nobody complained about nothin' we were doin' wrong about it.

When we was on the road in the camps, my daddy kept wine and whiskey for the workers. The farmer knew it. The police knew it. They wanted you to keep it cuz they don't want 'em in town.

We didn't run no kitchen. We didn't have time. Everybody bring their own food. Sometimes we'd have a guy who liked to cook. Everybody goes to that one guy and he cook it all.

I was fourteen years old when my mother left my father. I stayed there with him. I come from school, walked the fields, did the payroll.

In New York, the man says we're doing a good job. He offered my daddy a place up there. Like $3,000. Had about 104 acres of land and an old camp. It wasn't nothin' but old barns. We bought it, and about two years later he built a new labor camp on it. At that time, '66, '67, it was one of the best-looking labor camps in the state of New York. It still stands right today, but a lady got it leased up there. She's offerin' to buy it. She uses it for a horse farm. They raise a lot of horses around in there.

In 1985, my daddy told me, "You've been with me helpin' me. We're going to split down the middle."

So I take half the business. He stay here in Apopka with the crew and my sister. They ran that down here, and every penny I counted up, it came right down to the tee. Our gas money, our taxes, and the money we paid the people.

Crew Leader

I'll be sixty-seven the twenty-second of April and I'm still makin' it. I never drank, I never smoked, and I've been taken care of pretty good. A lot of the friends of mine, they died workin' on the muck day and night, out there and they sprayin'. I don't know if the chemicals caused them to die, but some became crippled or whatever.

I'm still a crew leader here in Apopka. I got a small crew now, about twenty workin' for me. That's all I wanna work. A crop come out once a year more'n likely. And whenever that crop come out, it got to be gathered. A lot of workers may not understand if the corn gotta be cropped today, you can't wait. The day after tomorrow it can be too hard.

I'm one of the highest payin' guys around here. I pay 'em $1.10 a field box starting the first fruit. Usually they pay startin' around $0.85 to $1.00.

The economy got so bad now it's hard. It's too tough. You can't make it now. Right back then, you could take $50 a week, a good week make you $1,500, $2,000, maybe $3,000. If you make $3,000 a week now, you gonna spend $2,000 to make it. It's more worse now than back then.

We gotta do workman's comp, the price of gas is high, and the insurance on your equipment, you ain't makin' no money. I got two fifteen-passenger vans, insurance on one of them cost $200 a month. I gotta have it whether you work or not. We've been off work now at least a month, but I still got to pay insurance on it.

And then bookkeeping, the payroll system thing. Back then, we do our own payroll. Now you pay a bookkeeper to take your taxes out, stay out of trouble with the government. I got them people doin' payroll and they make a mistake, they responsible for it. That what you payin' 'em for.

Apopka used to be a boomin' town years ago. You go back to the time, everybody want to come here. Nurseries goin', the muck goin', the grove, all of that. It was boomin', man. I never did think the time would get this bad. The citrus slow down, that was about a thousand jobs. You had GE and that muck. It was hard work, but they raised crops year-round in that muck, and people had work. The farmers, they sold out. The groves are freezin'. Young guys, they ain't goin' to the farm.

Lot of crew leaders depend on the Spanish folk. I've got a few Spanish guys. A few Asians, too. Lemme tell you 'bout the Spanish folk. They good. I got some that will work. But when they get situated, they gonna try to find themselves somethin' better. I don't blame 'em. I worked my way from the bottom to the top. My father and me worked the fields. I done pick oranges, and I know the feel of it. We one of the lucky ones.

10

"Education as the Way Out"

Mary Tinsley

Mary Tinsley is a poised, articulate, well-dressed woman who shocked me with her list of ailments. Calmly and authoritatively, she educated me about autoimmune diseases, lupus in particular. The body with lupus, it turns out, attacks healthy tissue, mistaking it for disease. Although many farmworkers suffer (or have died) from lupus, only recently have there been studies connecting the disease to the hazards of the profession.

In 2007, the NIH reported that "exposure to estrogenic organochlorine pesticides was associated with accelerated features of autoimmune disease in lupus-prone mice."[1]

In a March 18, 2011, article published in the *National Institute of Health Record*, Jan Ehrman writes about the findings of Dr. Christine Parks, a lead scientist of the National Institute of Environmental Health Sciences. Dr. Parks reported that "a new series of conditions referred to as autoimmune rheumatic disorders—lupus and rheumatoid arthritis (RA)—may also be linked to pesticide exposure."[2]

With a compassionate heart, Mary Tinsley has chosen to take what she has learned from her own disease and teach others. She currently works with the Lupus Foundation of Florida to reach minorities who suffer with lupus. She invites specialists to speak on topics such as applying for disability, the side effects of combining certain medications, and exercising without overdoing it.

Mary Tinsley. Photo by Gaye Kozanli.

I'm fifty-three years old, and I've been sick eighteen years. I felt dizzy all the time. I hurt. My joints were stiff. For a year and half, they couldn't figure out what was going on, and I started crying in the doctor's office. I said, "I feel just like my twin sister, Evelyn."

The doctor asked, "What's wrong with your twin sister?"

I said, "They said she has lupus."

That's when they decided to do an ANA (antinuclear antibody test) on me and found out I have lupus.[3]

Lupus is a very serious disease. It is more prevalent in African Americans, Hispanics, and Asians. Whites have it as well, but there's something about the disease that when we get it, it's harder on us and we die from it faster. They can't pinpoint why we suffer worse than someone else.

Right now, I have a morphine pump implanted. It's the only thing that controls my pain. They made a little incision in my abdomen area. They put a little device in there, and they put the medicine in it. There's a tube that runs into my back and the medicine drips into my spine to control my pain.

I go every four months, and they put new medicine in, and it really, really helps. Before that, I spent about ten years of suffering. I was taking eighteen pills a day for pain—Neurontin, Lyrica, morphine, hydrocodone. You can't function when you taking that kind of medication. It got to the point where it was so bad the medicine made me sick to my stomach, so I have gastroparesis.

I've had the steroid injections and nothing was working—nothing. The person you see now is not the person you would have seen years ago because that person years ago couldn't leave her house. The person years ago was sick—really sick—to the point of "Lord, I don't know if I want to be here."

Then the pain doctor told me about the pump, and it is a life saver. I don't have to take any other pain medicine. I got my life back. But there's a risk involved. It can cause you to become paralyzed if it slips out of place. The medicine has to drip onto your spine, but when it drips, nodules can build up. When it builds up, it can paralyze you. The good thing is, I go every four months and get checked. Right now, I'm having a lot of problem with my back, so when I see my doctor in two weeks, I'm going to request an MRI to make sure nothing is going wrong with this pump. That's all I can do.

Lupus can attack any part of your body from your eyes to your kidneys to your lungs to your heart to your skin. Your hair even falls out. It's really devastating because you have all kinds of problems. The medicine they treat you with is cancer medications. They just came up with a new drug. Been fifty years in the making, and we're hoping that it's going to be one of the great drugs that makes life so much easier for people having lupus.

The thing is, I didn't work on the farms as an adult, but I was exposed to the pesticides. When my mother was pregnant with me, she worked in the fields. My father was a farmworker all his life. His mom and dad worked the fields, and their parents worked the fields. My mother's side, her dad worked in the fields, but he never allowed his wife to work. She had to just stay in and raise seven children. So it's always been field work on both sides. They brought it home on their clothes, and during the weekends and summers I worked in the fields.

I remember a lot of times they would have this white stuff on the fruit, and my father would say, "Wash it off before you eat it because that stuff they spray for the bugs." Sometimes we kids did and sometimes we didn't.

Growing Up

My life was good and it was bad. It was good because there was love in our home. Also, I'm glad that my mother and father made sure we went to school and instilled in us to get an education. But it was hard because you were considered poor—that's the way people looked at you, poor. And you thought you were poor. You didn't have the money to go out and buy things.

My mother always got everything for us from the thrift store or from a garage sale. We didn't have a lot. She tried to make sure we were nice and clean, but we didn't have what some of our neighbors had who didn't have to go to the farms.

In my neighborhood, my parents and one other family went to the fields. Everybody else's parents had jobs working either in the hospitals or fruit-packing or in the nursing homes. We were the only family—myself and the family next to us—that went to the fields. So I was kind of embarrassed.

I'm blessed that my parents didn't make us work through the week. If we were out of school for a week, like for Christmas, we had to go. So while everyone else was enjoying their two-week Christmas vacation, we were at the grove. The days that it would rain, my sister and I would go, "Yay! Yay! Yay!" We would be so happy when it rained because we didn't have to go to the grove.

My brother didn't want to get scars on his skin from the pesticides, so he went out there when it was over one hundred degrees and he'd be all covered up—a long-sleeved shirt, gloves, a ski mask over his face. We used to laugh and say, "Frank, are you in there?"

That fruit bus would pick you up in your front yard to take you to the orange grove. You would have to get up and go. Your friends would see you get on that bus. And when we would get through, the bus would stop by the store so the people could cash their little checks. When I was eight, nine, ten, it didn't matter. Once I started getting eleven, twelve, then teenager, it started mattering because I didn't want the boys to see us looking like that.

My twin sister, Evelyn, and I hated getting out of the bus, going into the store. We'd be dirty, and we always had to have our heads tied up because we didn't want that stuff to get in our hair. We had on these clothes, and we just felt like when we went into the store, everybody knew we were fruit pickers. There were times when we would try, my sister and I, . . . we would take us soap and a rag and some change of clothes so we would wash off and at least look a little decent when we went inside the store. We would pretend we wasn't with the crew. We just in the store, like other people, getting what we want to get.

What I really hated was when the bus would wait until we got into Apopka, which is the town we lived in, and stop at that main store in Apopka.

My father would say, "Mary, you and Evelyn, why don't y'all go in there and get me an ice cream cone?" He loved ice cream cones.

I would play sick. I would say, "Oh, my stomach hurts. I feel bad." I didn't want to go in there because I didn't want the people to know I went to the fields on the weekends.

Sometimes our friends would pick at us. They would say in a sing-song voice, "Mary and Evelyn got to go to the fields. Mary and Evelyn got to go to the fields." So we didn't like it. No, I didn't like it one bit.

While our other friends were out playing on Saturday and Sunday, we were out in the grove picking fruit. And then if you had to go to the bathroom, you find yourself a spot behind one of the trees somewhere and hopefully there was nobody else thinking the same thing you were thinking. You made sure you took your paper out there, and after you went, you covered up. See how the cat do? That's how you do. I didn't like doing that.

I loved my father and I wasn't ashamed of him, but I sure hated the fact that he had to do it. He wasn't educated at all. My mother had a little education. She worked on the farms back in the '40s and '50s. She stopped working on the farms for a while and just did the going back and forth on what they called seasonal work. In the last ten years before they closed down the farms, she and my father both started working on the farms again doing the carrots.

I used to tell my brothers and my sister, I said, "We're going to get our education so we don't have to live like this, and we're going to make it possible that our mother and father don't have to work like this."

A lot of times we didn't want to go to the fields, and we would make up all sorts of excuses.

My daddy would say, "If y'all don't want to do this, you better go to school."

I remember one time my sister wouldn't go to school. She said, "I'm goin' to quit school."

My dad said, "Okay, you quit school."

And she did. She stopped for a while. But he made her go to the field every day. Didn't take her long to decide she'd better go back to school. So she graduated.

I remember one day my cousin and I needed some extra money for the fair. She said, "Let's go to the onion field."

I said, "Okay."

Well, I didn't realize how long those rows were. When we got through, we were all bent over. I was so sore, I couldn't even straighten up. My mother put me in the tub of hot water. Filled the tub up, and she put a certain amount of bleach in the water because back then there was a lot of people with a lot of rituals, and some said that the bleach would get the soreness out of you. I was sore for three or four days. I said, "Never again will I go to that kind of field."

I tried pickin' the cabbages because I wanted my own money. I didn't want to go to the grove because I hated the spiders and the lizards and the snakes that be running around in those groves. So I said, "Let's go pick some cabbages." But that's horrible, too. That was enough for me to say, "Mary, go to school, get some education. Get out of here. Get somebody that's going to make your life better than coming up."

When I got older and went into the service, I made sure I sent my money home. I would tell my parents, "Get whatever you want. You can put whatever you want in the bank for me." I wanted my parents to be able to pay their bills without feeling like they had to do all that. If my dad didn't feel like going to the grove on a Saturday or Sunday, he could stay home if he felt like it.

I thank God that a year before my dad died, they had stopped going up on the seasons. I just wish he would have been able to live longer to enjoy things better. When I got married, every year my husband and I would take a trip, and we always made sure my mother and father went to enjoy life. My father had never been down to the beach. But I made sure every Memorial Day weekend, we would take off on a Friday and stay the whole weekend. He loved it. All those years we had been to New York pickin' people's fruit, he had never been to Canada, he'd never been to New York City to see the Statue of Liberty. He had never done any of those things.

I tried my best to make sure my mother and father got a chance to experience some good things in life. Not just always workin' in the fields, workin' hard. Cuz that's some hard work. That's some *hard* work.

Up North

For six months of the year, we lived in Apopka. We spent the other six months in New York, where my parents picked apples. We were considered migrants. We would leave in June and get back about the end of November, right before Thanksgiving. I remember we would start school right after Thanksgiving, so we were already behind. We had to fit in when we got to our classroom. That was something that I hated—starting school that late in the year.

When my parents went up north for six months, we went to school up there. That was a little better because for some reason the people up north looked at us a little different than the southern people. On the way up north, we couldn't stop at some of the stores and eat in the restaurants. My parents would stop and grab some bologna and bread and some fruit or something. By the time you got to New York, you were constipated!

I was born in 1957. In the '60s in the South, there was still a lot of segregation, so a lot of the stores didn't want you to come through the front. You had to go through the back. Or they didn't want you to use their restroom. I don't know if our parents didn't want us exposed to that, so they never let us go in and see all that. I heard my parents talk about it after we got older. We never knew a lot of stuff that was going on.

Once we got in those northern states, you could stop in those restaurants. You could set there with the white and the black people. You could go use the bathroom. That's why we always say, "Why can't we live up here? Why can't we live up here?"

In New York, there was a big difference in the way you were treated than you were treated down south, yet we still had to live in the camps up north and we still had to go the outhouses. We didn't have a bathroom. The outhouse was a good little piece from the camp. When we got up in the middle of the night, we would have to use the slop bucket or go outside and find yourself a place and squat.

But the school system, that was better. They would come pick us up in front of the camp, which made us feel special. They did all kinds of field trips just for the migrants because I guess they wanted to show us things they felt we were missing. They would take us to see how they make glass. Take us to the cheese factory. Take us to the beach. Picnics. To the park. Takin' us to Rochester to the museums. Takin' us to the movie theaters. Gave us ice cream parties. Things that we wasn't exposed to.

We were much happier in the northern states than we were in the southern states. We felt like the people up there really care about us. It's like they were thinking, "These are migrants. They haven't had the good life like the people up north, so let's do good things for them." And they did. They really did. It was a big difference, I'm telling you.

When you went into the stores, the people just seemed like they were nicer, friendlier. Even when people went to town with their head scarves, the bandana things on their head, just coming from the fields, people wouldn't look at us funny.

They worked half a day in the apple field and get through at noon. At noon, you went into town to get your groceries and do your laundry because they didn't have laundromats on the camps. People would wash in the tubs, which my mom did, wash clothes in those foot tubs.

I think one problem is that at one time we were segregated in the South. I remember when we were in fifth grade there was integration and we went to the other side of the tracks to school. But when we was in New York, from the time I was in kindergarten, there was never any separation.

I stopped going up north when I was seventeen because the last year of high school, you have to be home. You can't stay six months up north and six months down here. You have to be home that last year of high school. So my father went, but my mom stayed home. That's what she did with every last one of her kids. If it was their last year in high school, she didn't go up north.

My mom looks back now and she says, "You know, Mary, I wished I had got a regular job maybe at a nursing home somewhere and worked and not went up north back and forth on the season, not worried about pickin' those fruits. Then I would have had a retirement."

Education and Work

That's what always motivated me, saying, "You know what? I'm going to go to school and get myself some education. I'm not going to be in those fields." I don't look down on the people that have to, but I just know that motivated me enough to know that I didn't want to go.

I went to Wymore Tech in Eatonville. When I graduated, I went into the service. I stayed six months in the full service and three years in the reserves. In the reserves, you go one weekend out of the month and two weeks in the summer. The service paid for me to go to West Side

VoTech in Winter Garden. I went there eighteen months and earned a certificate in a clerical office course.

After I finished, I got my first job, working for Orange County Mental Health Center over near Florida Hospital. I remember when I interviewed. I came back to the school and my teacher said, "If you really want to get that job, write that lady a letter and tell her how you appreciate her taking her time and interviewing you."

And I did that. She called me as soon as she got the letter and she said, "I just got through reading your letter. You're the only person that sent me a letter thanking me. I would like for you to come work for me."

I was clerk typist for seven social workers who worked for the county. We were assigned over at Florida Hospital, and they dealt with 3West patients, the ones that were mental. It was a locked unit. They had to do these psych-social histories on these patients that came through the hospital and then I typed them up. I had to go and get different doctors to sign the reports. They kept me busy, believe me.

I think I worked there about four years. Then I started working for the city of Winter Park, which I liked that. I worked in the Parks and Recreation Department. When people came in and they wanted to purchase cemetery plots or they wanted to use the different parks for weddings, I did that.

Then I worked for Travelers for eight years, and I would have loved to stay there, but I got sick. My memory started leaving. I couldn't remember anything. We were supposed to take only seven minutes to take a claim. It was taking me fifteen, twenty minutes because I had to keep repeating, "Say that again. What did you say?"

One day my boss listened on the other end, and when I got through talking, she called me into her office.

She said, "I was listening to you talk with the client." She said, "You constantly kept asking her to repeat herself. You're not supposed to have to do that. She shouldn't have to constantly repeat herself."

I couldn't explain why. Here I was for eight years getting perfect attendance on my job, getting outstanding evaluations, and all of a sudden I'm being called to the supervisor's office over and over, being yelled at about the mistakes I'm making. The mistakes, the mistakes, the mistakes. It was just overwhelming.

Then people who would see her constantly call me in the office, they were like, "What have Mary done?" They thought they was mistreating me. I thought they were mistreating me.

Then there were times when my hands would just freeze up. I was supposed to be typing, and they would go nowhere. Nowhere. I'm just trying to wait till these hands would move. Travelers tried to work with me as long as they could.

But I can understand. I was messing up. I was making some mistakes. As a matter of fact, I even took a year off, and then I came back and after about six months, they were like, "Mary, it's not going to work."

I had to stop working. When I went to get unemployment and I told them my story, they wouldn't even let me get unemployment. They said, "You need to be trying to apply for disability because to draw unemployment, you're going to need to be able to work." And that was a process by itself, too. It took forever. So it's just been a roller-coaster with me. Just a roller-coaster.

Diagnosed

I had been going to the doctor over a year and a half not knowing what it was. At one point, my doctor thought it was stress and sent me to a counselor. I did a six-week group counseling and then I did a six-week one-on-one counseling.

It wasn't until one of the therapists said to me, she said, "Miss Mary, if you feel there is something really wrong, don't let those doctors think that it's in your head." That stuck with me.

So I told my doctor at the time, "I'm not happy with the fact you're trying to say it's stress. It's not stress. There's something wrong with me, because every day it is something different."

And he was saying, "We sent you here, we sent you there. There's nothing coming back."

I remember when he sent me to the neurologist. The neurologist had seen me, and he put me on this medicine called Tegretol. It was seizure medication. Because at the time I was also having spasms in my legs like something was crawling up and down my legs all day. Never be still. I just wanted to beat that leg, so he tried me on that and that didn't work.

So the doctor said, "I don't know what else to give you."

That's when I started crying and told him about my sister. He said, "Have you ever told your primary doctor?"

Well, you know when you first go to the doctor, you fill out what your brother had, what your daddy had, your sister had. I had everything in there. If he'd looked in there, he mighta caught that.

So he says, "I'm going to have your doctor check you for lupus as soon as possible."

I didn't know what lupus was at that time. I just knew I lost my hair, I had black and blue bruises. I would wake up in the morning like somebody just beat me up. I got to the point that when I went to work, I wore long sleeves or a sweater because I didn't want people to think my husband was hitting on me. I would get the dry mouth and muscle aches.

My Husband

It's a good thing I have my husband. He said, "If I have to drop everything . . . if we don't go out to the restaurant to eat . . . I'm going to keep you in some insurance." And he did. He kept me in health insurance.

I met him roller skating. My sister and I wanted to move out of our parents' house, so we rented an apartment together. We became friends with these three guys who lived a little bit from our apartment. One of them was James. My sister and some other girls were out skating, and the three guys were there. James was messing around with my shoes, and I noticed a guy come in.

I said, "Ooh, I like the way he looks." I said, "I wouldn't mind getting to know him."

James said, "Hey, that's my cousin Bruce. You want me to introduce y'all to him?"

I said, "Yeah, go ahead." And he introduced us.

Bruce didn't like me right away. He talked to me, but he didn't like me. Then he said, "Would you like to go out sometime?"

I said, "Sure."

He said, "I'm not lookin' to get serious about anybody."

And I said, "Well, I'm not looking to get serious about anybody." I did like him, but I didn't tell him that I liked him.

We dated. He said, "I'm going to be dating other people, so I just want you to know that." And he did.

But the end of it all, we did get together, and we got married. We've been married thirty-two years. The twenty-fifth of August will be thirty-two years we've been married.

He's been a good husband to me. We bought our first house in Orlando. I waited three years until I had my daughter. Two years after she was born, that subdivision started goin' down. Everybody in the world, dope dealers to you name it, moved in there.

One day my husband went to the convenience store nearby and somebody pulled up right in front of our little girl and asked if he wanted to buy drugs.

My husband came home. He said, "We are moving." He said, "I'm not having my daughter raised up around this. We're moving." He said, "I don't even want to live in this city. I want to move into the country."

Our parents had an old house. They let us rent it from them. We stayed there five years, saved a lot of money, bought two and a half acres of land out in the country in Zellwood. Then we built our house. We've been living there ever since.

We have one daughter. We instilled in her when she was coming up "Go to school, get your education." When she was a little girl, I put her in Florida Prepaid college fund. Education is a must. There's no ifs, ands, buts about it. We said, "You cannot stay in this house and not do well." I know there were many days she got mad at me. Get home from school. I said, "Turn that TV off. Do your homework."

She's twenty-seven years old now. She's a nurse, and she bought herself a townhouse.

My husband has been so good to me. If he comes home and there's no dinner because I haven't been feeling well, he'll just make a sandwich. If I feel like cooking, it's okay. If I don't, it's okay. He'll tell me, "Don't wash the clothes until I'm home and I'll help you wash them." Sometimes I'll feel good, and he'll get home and he'll say, "I thought I told you to wait until I get home."

I'll say, "Well, I was feeling good."

He says, "But maybe your back will start hurting tonight."

My husband made sure he took care of us. He's worked for Florida Hospital for thirty-five years, ten of those as a respiratory therapist.

At first his employer didn't want to put me on his insurance because of preexisting problems with lupus. I kept the COBRA until they approved for me to go onto his plan. By that time, Medicare kicked in. So Florida Hospital is my primary and Medicare is my secondary. That covers a lot of medical bills. I would probably be broke from all the co-payments if I had to pay all of that money out of my pocket, but I don't.

Insurance and Health Care

But then you have people with lupus who can't afford to go to the doctor. What about the people like my girlfriend Johanna? She had to stop working because they found out she had lupus. She has kidney involvement, but she can't go to the doctor, because she doesn't have any insurance. What's she gonna do? Her kidneys are failing.

She said she went to the clinic. They told her she didn't qualify. She does get a disability check, but you have to be on disability two years before Medicare will kick in. So next year, Medicare will kick in. She'll be able to go to the doctor to see about herself. But that's next March before that happens. So in the meantime she's just struggling. When she gets really, really sick, she'll go to the emergency room. They'll put her in the hospital a couple days, a week, get her all straightened out. She's worried about all the bills that she's accumulating from the disease.

They have to do a specific test to diagnose lupus, and most doctors don't do that. That's why a lot of times people who suffer with lupus like myself have to go years of suffering or they're almost in the hospital at the point of death before they realize something's not right. Lupus mimics so many things. One minute your joints are hurting, then you have a headache or you have a rash on you.

It's the same with my twin sister. She also has an autoimmune disease, and she has Medicaid. She started twenty years ago. We would be somewhere and she would just pass out. And then after that, she started walkin' funny. People in the neighborhood would say, "Oh, since when did Evelyn start becoming an alcoholic?" That's what people thought—that she was drunk. And then she went to the doctor and the doctor noticed a skin rash. They first diagnosed her with lupus, but a year later they said it wasn't lupus. They said it was psoriasis.

She also has something that deteriorates the brain stem. Her speech.

You can barely make out what she's saying. She can't walk by herself anymore. With the Medicaid insurance, she can only see the Medicaid doctors. A lot of tests and expensive things they just didn't do.

It just so happened that my sister has a very good doctor now that says, "I'm going to request all of these tests be done." She's been suffering with this, and she's getting worse.

I have private insurance so I can pretty much get better health care. I see a neurologist. I see a rheumatologist. I see a pain doctor. I have a primary doctor. I have a nephrologist. I have a gastrologist. At one time I had a dermatologist cuz my hair came out. With lupus, your hair will come out. A lot of people with lupus wear wigs because it does attack your hair follicles. People think that you have cancer. Once you start takin' all the medicine to control the disease, that affects your hair, too.

I take a medicine called Plaquenil where I have to go every six months to the ophthalmologist to check my eyes because Plaquenil causes irreversible eye damage. It will cause you to go blind. For an hour and a half, they test me. I mean they give me all kinds of different tests, and if there's any changes in my retina, that doctor gonna check it. And if it's Plaquenil, they gonna take me off of it.

Right now I'm dealing with my knees. I have no cartilage in my knees. The bone rubbin' against the bone, but I'm getting injections. As long as the injections work, I'm just going to deal with that. If that doesn't work, I'll do the gel. When the gel stops working, then we'll talk about knee replacement surgery, but right now I'm just going to deal with the shots.

There are people whose skin looks like it's burnt. It's not a pleasant sight, believe me. That's when it's active. The doctors that you go to try to monitor you. They try to keep the lupus suppressed, because as long as it's suppressed, you're fine. When it's active, you don't know what it's going to do. You don't know if it's going to attack your heart. You don't know if it's going to attack your lungs. You don't know if it's going to attack your eyes.

But I've been blessed. I haven't had any real major organ problems. The only problem I had was my pancreas, and I had to spend a week in the hospital. But that's it. My major problem is the chronic pain. My joints, my muscles. There are times when I cannot get out of the bed by myself. Then there are days when I can jump up, clean my whole house, run all over the place.

I get a little steroid in me, I can do flips. I don't like to take the steroids too much. If you take the steroids too much, you can gain a lot of weight. Within a six-week period, I gained forty pounds. I'm not lyin' to you. You get a moon face. They call it moon face because it get round and puffy and your joints all swollen. You can't just stop taking it. A lot of the medicine we take, you can't just stop takin' it, but you can wean off of it.

Lupus Foundation of Florida

I said, "Lord, if you ever help me to do better, then I want to help somebody else." The Lupus Foundation wanted a minority outreach started, so we started it. It was myself and three other African American ladies. I have a good support system. Everybody doesn't. That's where the Lupus Foundation comes in as far as having a support group to try to lift people up. Try to encourage them. You can go and talk to other people, and maybe there's something I can suggest that might help you. Maybe there's something you may share that could help me. That's what we do. We have a round table, and we talk about what we're going through.

There's eight of us that meet on a regular basis; six of 'em was exposed to the pesticides. They worked on the farms or in the nurseries that was around the farms.

We meet every month at the Farmworker Center. Sometimes I get speakers—a doctor to speak or a lawyer—because a lot of people trying to get disability. I've had people like aerobic people to come to show us ways to exercise without overdoing it. I had a pharmacist to tell us how to properly take our medicine. When you have a lot of medicine, you wonder, "Why my stomach hurting so bad?" Certain medicines shouldn't be taken together, and a lot of people didn't know that. So now I space my medicines about. We have some people who just grabbed the whole thing and throw it in their mouth and take it. I can't do that. If I do, my stomach is just on fire.

Of the four who started the support group, I must say, I'm the only one standing.

Tracey passed away at a really young age. Charlene really got sick where she couldn't come to the office. She had had kids, and she was high risk.

And Lola. Lola worked on the farms. Her mom worked on the farms. It was Lola and myself left trying to run the office a couple days out of the week. One day she had met me at the office on a Monday, and I said, "Lola, your legs are so swollen. What's wrong? You've got so much inflammation."

She said, "I don't know what's going on." She said, "Let's meet Wednesday so we can go through these drawers and get through all of this unnecessary paperwork."

I said, "Well, okay."

That Wednesday, ten o'clock I got there. No Lola. Ten thirty, no Lola. Eleven o'clock, no Lola. I said, "Well that's strange. Lola always be on time." I called her house.

Her mother say, "Mary, can't talk. Lola, we rushin' her to the hospital." From the neck down, she couldn't do anything.

She's in a wheelchair now. She ended up with myasthenia gravis. It's where the muscles just shut down. For the first few months, she had to be fed baby food. She had to be bathed. She had to be taken care of. Everything. She was in a nursing home. After a while in that nursing home, she got depressed, because every time they put a senior in the room with her, they would die. She's home now. She can move her arms. She can't walk. She's in a wheelchair. She doesn't come into the office. I do the office by myself. But she works from the house. She does all the 1-800 numbers. When people call, she calls everybody back. She will come to the meetings, because she can catch the Lynx bus, and she helps me when I do health fairs. So she still tries to stay as active as she possibly can.

We almost lost her back in November. She went to the doctor. They sent her immediately to the hospital. By the time she got there, she coded. She don't remember anything for about two months later. She was in a coma. They had to put her in a coma because her heart and lungs were not working. I would go see her, and I would start crying. I would get so upset because I was thinking I was losing my friend. We've been together for years, working together, and here she's fighting for her life.

I remember her mom saying that they told her just to prepare. But she has a strong mother. Her mother said, "I'm not preparing for my daughter's death. I'm not going to believe or accept what y'all saying."

I told her mom, I said, "If you can believe, I can believe. We're going to believe the best."

She made it home. It was some months later, but she made it home. The lupus damaged her lungs so much that now she's not really a candidate for a lung transplant. She's on oxygen. I don't know what's going to happen if those lungs . . . go . . . because she's not eligible for a lung transplant. Not now. It's too bad.

The sad thing about lupus is having people that you know and then they die. I've seen a lot of people die. I've been at the hospital bed of a lot of my friends that have lupus that have died.

I know I'm blessed because I thought at one time I wouldn't be around to raise my daughter, but God did spare my life. God's been good to me. I won't complain.

I was ashamed to be a migrant. I always told God, "I don't want to do that kind of work again." And I've never really had to.

But I never would put anybody else down. Matter of fact, I understand these people that work on these farms now and do the carrots and the onions and whatever else. When I pass by going towards Astatula, they got a lot of farms on both sides and I see people out there working. It's just too bad they don't get the money that they should get or they don't make it better for them. Cuz that's a lot of work. It really is.

When I pass by, I'm like, "Oh, God, give 'em strength. God, give 'em strength."

11

"I Never Will Forget It"

Betty Dubose

The first time I interviewed Betty, Geraldean was present. When I asked a question, Geraldean jumped in, talking, describing, and reveling in long stories, while Betty sat with a faraway look in her eye. When Geraldean sang the old slave songs the farmworkers used as code, Betty joined in, a quiet accompaniment to Geraldean's lusty rendition.

I felt that behind that faraway look were stories that only Betty could tell, so I asked permission to return when it would be only the two of us. On my second visit, Betty relayed her haunting stories slowly. I did not interrupt her pauses, and she gained momentum.

I learned how the death of Betty's mother affected her: "It is a hard thing to lose your parents. Only God can heal you from it. I know because I'm a livin' witness. I didn't think I was gonna make it when my mama died. But I made it through God. You don't get but one mama in this lifetime. One mama in this lifetime and you'd better know how to treat her."

I learned how she felt working on the muck as an adult: "I'll be wantin' to quit, but I can't quit because I have to feed my children. Have to keep goin'. Have to keep cuttin.'"

I learned the two things she is most proud of: "I'm most proud that I raised my children. Worked hard and bought me a house. Hope and pray to God for me to pay it off. I think I owe $16,000 more on it. I've been here almost

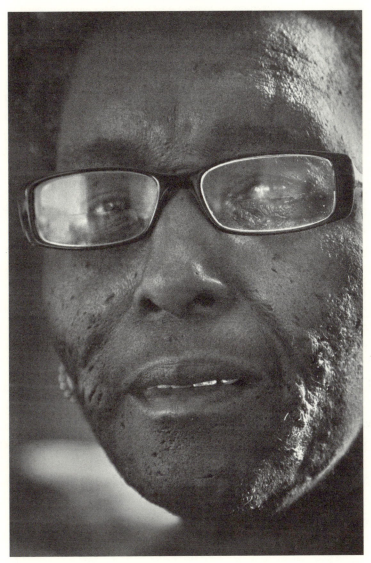

Betty Dubose. Photo by Gaye Kozanli.

twenty-four years. The twenty-third of this month will be twenty-four years."

What emerged was the picture of a strong woman with high ethical standards. She earned the scars on her face and the scars in her heart through a lifetime of hard work, and she holds her head high as she says, "We fed America."

My daddy brought us to Apopka from Alabama when I was six months old. My mama used to leave my daddy, go back to Alabama, come back to Florida, leave my daddy, go back to Alabama, come back to Florida. So the whole family went back to Alabama for a while. I think we left in 1962. Yes, had to be '62. I was up there when Kennedy was shot.

My grandma and grandpa was in the cotton field, and they heard the president got shot. All of them come to runnin' out of the cotton field. I was about eight or nine years old, and I was at the house, but I remember. They went to cryin'. I was sad because I seen them cryin'.

I said, "Why you be cryin'?"

They said, "It gonna be rough."

Cuz it already be rough, and they had a president that would help them. Help the blacks. They killed him. It was November 22, 1963. A lot of fear in 1963.

I never will forget it.

I worked in pesticide all my life. I was eight years old pickin' cotton in Alabama, and they had pesticides. They plant the cotton seed with it. It was pink, and when it dries, it stick in your finger. I hated workin' in the cotton field. It grow in a boll and it bloom out. You pick it out with your bare hands. You had a sack on you to put the cotton in.

We come back to Apopka, Florida, when I was ten years old, and I started workin' on the muck farms on the weekends cuttin' leaf lettuce. I had a big butcher knife. Sometimes I got injured. Just wrap it up with tape and kept on workin' because I had to work. Had to make ends meet.

At that time, my mama had six children. I got a older brother than me. I'm next to my older brother. My mama had seven more after me. Yes, she did.

We had to work to help feed 'em. Me and my brothers and sisters, we did it for years. My mama wasn't working, but my daddy was working. And we helped out every weekend. We made $10 a day.

For a while, my daddy was a crew leader in the orange grove. They had pesticide there, too. I was pickin' oranges at ten years old. It was hard work. Real hard work. When the orange crop over, we go to the muck. See what I'm sayin'? We go from the muck to the orange back to the muck. Always in the pesticide.

I 'member once when I was not thirteen years old. We used to be down in those orange groves. And oh, God, did we work. They were payin' 35¢ a box. One time, we worked so hard and we was comin' home from the grove and a trailer overturned. All the oranges dumped out onto the road. We was already tired. Had worked so hard, my stomach fell down. My grandmama, she put a rag around my stomach to pull it back up. They know how to do something to pull it back up, and I got a little better. We had to pick up them oranges off the road for 25¢ a box and put them back on the trailer.

I never will forget it.

I went to eighth grade at Phillis Wheatley Elementary School, an all-black school. Then they came in and started mixing up the children together, desegregated the schools. I stopped and went to work. I liked school. I chose to go to work because there was a lot of work that needed to be done to help feed my brothers and sisters. I told my daddy I wanted to stop going to school and go to work. I went to work full-time at that time. I was fifteen picking oranges with my daddy.

I hated pickin' oranges. That was so hard work. Oh, man. My daddy used to shake 'em on the ground, and we pick 'em up. You had to tote them big old sacks and pick the oranges off the ground. Put them in the bin.

When I was sixteen, I put my age up to eighteen and worked at Plymouth Citrus, where they grade oranges.

Then I went to Alabama with my auntie. They had come to Florida to visit, and I went back with them. I got pregnant, and I was workin' in the fields with the pesticides. I carried him six months, and he was stillborn. I got pregnant again, still workin' in the fields. I carried him seven months, and he was stillborn.

In '73, I didn't work on the farms. I was nineteen. I had a hefty baby boy. Seven pounds, three ounces. I had him in Tuskegee, Alabama, in a hospital on the campus of a black college. I come back to Florida after that and went back to workin' in the fields. I had five more children, all very low birth weights.

My daughter Terry, she weighed three pounds, six ounces. Marcus weighed two pounds, thirteen ounces. LaToya weighed five pounds, nine ounces. Lastly, I had a set of twins. One weighed three pounds, fifteen ounces, and one weighed three pounds, ten ounces.

The twins I had at seven months. I was workin'. It was a Wednesday, and my feet were swolled up this big. I could hardly make it.

My boss man said, "You need to stop workin' now, don't ya?"

I said, "I'm trying to work till Wednesday so I can get my money on payroll."

I worked until Wednesday, then I stopped. On that Monday, I went into labor. I had the twins. I ain't know I was pregnant with twins. Both of them had to stay in the hospital. I got them out one by one. One of them had a real breathin' problem when she was born.

One of them died when she was three months old. I used to get up every morning and fix the bottles. I had some Flintstones bottles, and I put them in a pot to warm them up. I come back. I see them layin' in the bed, and I didn't pay no attention. My baby was layin' face down. Said she died of a crib death. I like to went crazy. It was thirty-two years ago.

I never will forget it.

I got five living children. All of 'em got learning disabilities except one—the one I had when I was *not* workin' in the muck.

The muck looked like black dirt. I mean real, real black dirt. Open field. No trees to get up under when it's hot. We sang and cut and sang songs and keep on workin'.

I had to go to the field at five in the morning, and we'd cut by car light. Shine the light in the field so to see how to cut. I got up at four o'clock, got ready to be in that field by five to cut by the car light. We'd be way up that field by the time they come back for the boxes. We'd have something for them in the packin' house.

It'd be hot, and we cuttin'. Airplanes be sprayin' the fields. It'd be flyin' and sprayin' that stuff right on top of us. That stuff just like some sticky on ya. Sprayed pesticides right on top of us. They knew. Yes, they did. Didn't care. All they wanted was for us to work and get that order out. For years they did that.

My daddy worked on the muck until he died of cancer. He was fifty-one years old. He wasn't sick for no long time. I'd say he was sick for about six months. They cut all of his stomach out. We thought they was sending him home because he got better, but they were sending him home to die.

A lot of people gone on that worked on the muck. I've seen a lot of people pass away. Cancer. Ate up with cancer. Lot of 'em gone on. Young people dyin'. I know a lady her whole family died workin' on that muck. They get killed or they die. Another lady, all her boys worked on the muck, and every last one of them died. And one daughter. I think about five or six of them boys. Two of them got killed, though, I know. The oldest boy had a sunstroke out there on that muck. Died. They have one brother left. He's real sick now. Real sick.

My mama was a couple years older than my daddy. She always have a cup beside the bed spittin' in it. Like something was in her throat. I believe she was sick from the pesticide because she used to wash our clothes from the chemicals on that muck farm. Most all of my brothers and sisters worked on that muck farm, come home, and Mama used to wash our clothes. She don't have no washing machine either. She used to wash 'em by hand.

After my daddy died, my mama still had two or three children at home. My baby brother, he took care of my mama until she passed away in '95. All of us pitched in.

Then my brother took up and passed away. He worked in the farm and the nursery, too. He passed away in 2003. He was about thirty-nine. Not quite two years later, I had another brother pass away. He worked on the fields, too. Cancer.

I lived in the quarters. They used to call it the Graveyard Quarters because the graveyard was next to the houses. Most of the people who lived there worked on the muck farms or the orange groves. The man who owned them did not own the farms. He just rented those houses down there. His name Mr. McCormack. The rent was $10 a week. He paid the light bill and the water bill. Stayed down there for years.

We had a juke down there. We called it the Graveyard Juke. We used to hang out. We used to have a lot of fun there. Then someone comin' in there raisin' Cain. Lot of people got killed down there. Get in fights. Get their gun and stuff. I wasn't there, but I'd hear about it. We used to play music all the time. Piccolo. People would be dancing. I went there every weekend. I don't think they have those any more, the juke joint.

I worked on the farm for years and years, twenty-seven years. I remember we used to work so hard on that muck out there, and it'd be rainin'. Rainin' so hard you could hardly see, and that man come down through the field, the boss man come down through the field, because he needed that order out.

He said, "Y'all go ahead and work. Work and I'll give y'all extra."

We went for it. We worked in that rain. It'd be pourin' down. To get that extra money. I didn't see that much extra nowhere. But we worked in that rain a lot of time cuz he wanted to get that order out. And we got it out. We used to be out there in them fields. In that rain. Cuttin'. Cuttin' that leaf lettuce. You had to crawl on your knees to cut leaf lettuce.

I never will forget it.

I'd crawl all the way down the field and cut. Take and hold it over and cut and stack it up. Just cut, cut, and keep cuttin'. Stack it on the side row. Someone come behind you to pack it. We was workin' as a team. I cut and someone behind me would pack it. I did about four rows down, and if we weren't finished with the order, we'd turn around and do more rows. Depend on what type of order he have to get out. I don't know how many heads of lettuce I cut. Just cut it, stack it, and keep goin'. Did it for years.

I worked piece time. Everybody workin' together. We called it "cuttin' across the board." Everybody cut together, and then the money we make, we divide it between and pay each one of them off. You had to keep goin' in order to make anything. The whole crew, everybody in the field was "cuttin' across the board." I could take four rows and somebody take two rows, but we'd all be even.

Everybody on the crew do something out there. We had a box maker to make the boxes. It was a flat box, just put them together. They'd pull the truck down the rows as we cut. The boxes on top of the truck. They'd make the boxes and throw them out.

Next, somebody cuttin'. That's what I did. We cut it and lay it on the side. Just keep on cuttin' up the field. I crawled all the way. No way in the world I could have stood over that stuff to cut cuz the stuff too low on the ground. Crawlin' all day long.

I used to cut all the way up so the packer won't be at my back. I cut fast so I can get a head start, then I take a little breather. It'd be so hot, I'd wear a sweatshirt. I sweat, that sweatshirt keep me cool. We had these plastic gloves we wore, but I didn't wear them much. I didn't like 'em. Had to have my bare hands.

After me, somebody packin' the leaf lettuce into crates. Then the loaders come up and pick up the crates and put 'em in the truck. So if you look ahead, empty crates in the field. If you look behind, filled crates in the field and the trucks pickin' 'em up. My daddy used to work pickin' the boxes up in the field.

We used to have rain pants on to work in. Looked like a raincoat. Yellow, rubbery. Like overalls but they was like a raincoat. I 'member one time, a lady from Belle Glade, we was cuttin' leaf stuff, and a snake jumped inside her rain pants! She come runnin' out of those rain pants hollerin', "Snake! Snake!" Probably a moccasin because that's all that was in those canals. I went to runnin' like I don't know what. I was shakin' and scared the rest of that day.

Another lady named Dolly May, we were cuttin' one time and she hit a snake and threw him in the canal. I said, "Good God Almighty!" She cut its head off and threw him in the canal. See, if you were workin' right beside that canal, see what I'm sayin', those snakes come out of that canal. That was a moccasin. She kept cuttin'. I said, "Oh my God. I can't handle this." She said she saw them all the time and cut 'em up and threw them in the canal. I didn't see no snakes. If I'd'a seen a snake, tha'd'a been it.

We brought our own lunch, but there was nowhere to wash your hands at. Sometimes we cooked the night before. We brought leftovers. If I was workin' on the mule train, I'd keep my lunch on the mule train. But in the fields, they had a truck come behind you. The van. We'd go back to the van and eat. We didn't have much time. You had to eat when you knock off because we were still tryin' to get that order out. Get the order out and then you eat.

After we do the crops on the muck, I go back to the nursery. They had pesticides out there also. Either way it went, I was in pesticides.

That's what happened to my face.

They had just sprayed the plants, and we thought it was safe to go back in there. They *say* it was safe to go back in there, so we went back in and started workin'. That stuff splashed in my face, and it burned. I started having big knots coming, so I went to the hospital. I stayed in the hospital four days. They said it was from the pesticide. I was on workman's comp.

Even when I come back and went back to the nursery, my face was burning, so I just quit.

In the nursery, I was a dish garden maker most of the time. Used to stick plants in beautiful bowls and ship them out. They have beds of plants, and you go out to the beds and cut the plants and bring them back there to stick them in the pots for it to grow into a big philodendron or something like that.

They called the nursery the Fundry. I did that for ten years.

I'd take a leave of absence and go out to the muckland. That's how I worked it so I won't be out of work. Muck to the Fundry.

The contractor, he drive into the field in a big, new truck. He get out, cut a piece of lettuce, look at it, and get back in his truck. He don't want that stuff, that pesticide, in his face. He don't stay but five minutes, get back in his air-conditioned truck, and drive away.

A lot of 'em gone that worked on the muck. Lot of 'em. Many of them had a bad cough. Real bad cough they used to have. Like emphysema. Couldn't hardly breathe. Cough like something in your throat all the time.

They closed the farms now. Lake Apopka contaminated. The airplanes spray those fields. They had pesticides in their planes spraying that stuff over the fields and over us. They draw water out of that lake. The pesticide rise up, you know what I'm sayin'? It's in that lake. I remember it happening. All them birds died and all them fish. They workin' on the Lake Apopka instead of the people. They been tryin' to conserve that darn lake and people sick and dyin'.

After twenty-seven years doing farmwork, I left to work in a nursing home. I was doing custodial work. I said, "Lord have mercy, I wish I had knowed this here when I worked all them years on that farm. I coulda been workin' in this here nursing home." I liked that. I didn't work there but six months because I hurt my feet. I said, "All these years I worked in that nursery, and I coulda been workin' in here."

I'd be in the room with them older people, and they'd tell me stories. I just sit there and listened. One said her niece brought her there and ain't never come back in all those years. Six years she hadn't seen her.

I said, "You mean to tell me that woman left you here and didn't come back?"

The stories they could tell you. I could sit there and cry. How could you leave your mama and your aunt in some place like that and don't come back to see about 'em?

Now I takin' care of other people's children. My son was datin' this girl. She had a daughter by him, and the state took her children, a boy and a girl. One was one year old, and the other was three. I went and got 'em.

The other one ain't no kin to me, but I raised him anyway just as like he was mine. Yesterday he turned eighteen. I throwed him a party. We had collard greens, ribs, fried chicken, and potato salad. He wanted soul food, so I cooked him soul food.

I adopted them. I heard they can get a college degree, so I adopted 'em so they could get that college degree. They got a four-year scholarship. If they call it in.

Both of 'em actin' up.

I said, "God already blessed you with a scholarship. What more do you want? You got to learn how to do things in order to go with that scholarship. Now you say you want to be an architect. I say you got to go to school. You've got the money to go. But you want to choose to be out there with your friends actin' silly."

I talked and talked and talked and talked. Done made a record of it. Talkin', talkin', talkin', but they choose to do what they want to do. Know what I'm sayin'?

I leave it in the hands of God. Let Him work it out because He know what I done done.

I help my two sons. They are out of work. Unemployment is gone. They don't have anything. Ain't no money coming in. Ain't gonna let them go hungry if I can help it. No way.

It's been a rough road. By God, I made it. And I'm still makin' it, by His grace. I have faith in God, yes, I do. He's still on the scene even though what we went through.

Things will come to pass because God knows who was in those fields. *We* was in those fields. We put food on America's table all those years. Now we sick, and we have cancer.

I never will forget it, and neither will God.

12 *"Improving the Lives of Others"*

Tirso Moreno

All former farmworkers whose stories appear in this book are members of the Farmworker Association of Florida (FWAF). Tirso Moreno is the cofounder and general coordinator of the organization. I had a hard time scheduling an interview with Tirso since he spends the bulk of his time traveling between the five branches spread out over thirteen counties. As a result, he became my last interviewee. Tirso spoke candidly, almost without stopping, for over an hour. I learned not only the history and current work of FWAF but the heart of the man who was instrumental in its origin.

Tirso was a farmworker laboring in a grove owned by Minute Maid. He had good working conditions, wages, and benefits. He looked around and realized that was not the case for the vast majority of the estimated three hundred thousand farmworkers in Florida. He says, "I just thought that if we can have that, why the others cannot have it."

He began working with a small group of farmworkers in Mascotte, Florida, some thirty-five miles southwest of Apopka, with the aim of organizing them to lobby more effectively for better wages, housing, and working conditions. In 1986, he left his job to help found FWAF, dedicating his efforts full-time to helping others have a better working environment. The guiding vision of the organization is to create "a social environment where farmworkers' contribution, dignity, and worth are acknowledged, appreciated, and respected through economic, social, and environmental justice."[1]

A handful of FWAF's major accomplishments include:

1. Successful passage of the Farmworker Transportation Safety Act in 2006 requiring seatbelts in vans transporting farmworkers
2. Participation in three community-academic farmworker health research projects with state universities
3. Creation of the Lake Apopka Dislocated Workers Program, in which community members reached out to over 1,200 farmworkers to address retraining/reemployment and housing relocation needs
4. Formation of the community-generated Lake Apopka Farmworkers Environmental Health Survey project with community members, which interviewed 148 former farmworkers impacted by pesticide exposure
5. Active participation in the National People of Color and Indigenous People Environmental Leadership Summits, the United Nations World Conference against Racism, two World Social Forums, and the Southeast Social Forum

Although there have been great improvements, as Tirso says, "farmworkers still suffer a lot of injustice, exploitation, [and] discrimination," and "we have to continue working to improve living and working conditions for our fellow farmworkers."

My father was a United States citizen, but his parents moved from Texas into Mexico around the time of the First World War, and they stayed there. They kept their citizenship, but they told him, "Never go back to the U.S." I assume that was because they sent you to war in the front of the line, and when it is time to come home, you were at the back of the line.

My father was a farmer in Mexico. We were in a hurricane. He lost everything in the farm, animals and everything. He moved into town and took a job. He used his body to load things. He was doing what he

Tirso Moreno. Photo by Gaye Kozanli.

knew how to do to support a family. He wanted to be a professional, but he didn't have the resources to go to school. He didn't have enough money to support a family of eleven. He said, "Better to be a farmworker in the U.S. than a farmworker in Mexico."

In the 1940s, he came back to the U.S. undocumented for about ten years. He was H-2A.[2] Because he had to support a large family, he had to do what he was asked not to do—claim for his citizenship. I mean he started using the documents he had, but he was not allowed to come across the border until he hired an attorney and got a U.S. passport.

Then we came following him. Because of his income in farmwork, we were limited to bring two by two until he brought all the family. It took many years. I was a teenager when I first came here. I got married five or six years later, when I was about twenty-three. By the time I got married, I think only four of us had migrated. At the end, because some of us would help with the income, he brought in my mother and the others to Florida.

My wife was undocumented for seven years. I was a permanent resident, not a U.S. citizen. Permanent residents that work here are documented, but you apply for your wife or children. You have to get in line, because there is a limit of how many people can migrate from Mexico. There is a purpose for that, I guess. It's a control by some people who want control.

My wife and I came to Orange County, Florida, in 1976 with our child to work in harvesting oranges for Minute Maid when they used to have groves here. A friend of mine and myself moved into assisted farmworker housing in South Apopka. It was 1982, something like that. There were no Latinos in the South Apopka neighborhood at that time. We were the two Mexican families moving into the African American neighborhood. Then about two years later, I bought a house in the same neighborhood. That is the actual address where we live now.

While we were working in Minute Maid, my wife became very active in the local Minute Maid union in Apopka. I became the president of the Ranch Committee. I moved into the vice president position voluntarily because I wanted that position to organize other people to improve their working conditions and their wages. Before Minute Maid, I was working not under a union contract for a long time. I felt bad about seeing all of the people suffering.

I mean, with labor contractors, they don't allow us to say how you feel, because if you don't like it, you can leave. They fire you or they punish you. At Minute Maid, we had better benefits than other farmworkers have ever seen. We had better wages and better working conditions.

For several years, I was volunteering union activities and I also worked picking oranges. I tried to organize other farmworkers not with much success. We were trying to import an organizing style from California.

There was a lady who worked in the union with us a season or two. She was a volunteer under United Farmworkers (UFW). We kind of built up a relationship. She knew what I think, and she liked it. I didn't know she was a millionaire. Her father was one of the founders of UPS. She left to get married but with some sentiments about the farmworkers getting organized and improving things.

I met the nuns who were working for the Catholic Diocese of Orlando.[3] They had a ministry helping the farmworkers. They invited me to church. I'm not a religious person. I still don't go to church every Sunday. I consider what I do and practice my religion.

The summer of 1983, the nuns offered me a job as a professional organizer. I was doing something similar for years but not as a way of living. I wasn't sure I could do it as a job. Every year, my wife and I used to go up north to work in the summer and come back. So that year we signed up for unemployment and stayed here. I became a volunteer for the nuns for the summer. A month later, around the time the season was going to start, the nuns wanted me to respond to them if I wanted to be employed as the lead to organize the farmworkers in the area.

I always thought that I couldn't be happy with all the benefits if other people didn't have them, too. I wanted other people to also live better, so I accepted the job. I worked for the nuns for three years. Years later, I found out the millionaire who volunteered in the orange grove paid for my salary for those three years.

After that, in 1986, I helped found the Farmworker Association of Central Florida. The name was later changed to the Farmworker Association of Florida. At that time, it was just a local small operation in parts of Orange and Lake Counties. Right now it touches thirteen counties.

I was not a professional. You are called "professional" when you do a job for business purposes, making money, and you have a lot more training. I learned by doing things and attended some trainings.

When we founded the FWAF here in Apopka, we had Latinos, African Americans, and Haitians. In the 1960s and '70s, the majority of the farmworkers were black—either African American from other states in the South or African descendants from the Caribbean. Most of the Latinos were U.S. citizens or permanent residents from South Texas and northern Mexico. And, of course, there were Anglos from the Appalachian region.

By the '80s, the number of Latino farmworkers had grown up, and a lot of them were undocumented. In 1986, there was a decision made at the Congress level to do a legalization for the undocumented farmworkers. When that legal decision happened, that was a big thing for our community. We started giving out information to the community, dealing with the interpretation of the new law and dealing with the INS [Immigration and Naturalization Service, currently known as Immigration and Customs Enforcement].

We found out that there was a big community of Mexicans in Volusia County, and they didn't have any information about legalization. Then we found out the fern workers were not considered farmworkers because ferns were not classified as a perishable product. Most of the workers in the ferneries were undocumented. We went there, we gave out information, we set up an office there, and that became the fourth chapter. There's a whole history of inclusion of the fern cutters on the interpretation of the law. Some big fights, but FWAF won three lawsuits for fern cutters. Now they are covered under the Agricultural Worker Protection Act.

In the early '90s, we formed a chapter in Homestead and another in Immokalee. The last chapter we formed has been in Fellsmere since 2004 after a second hurricane hit the town. We went there to help the community push for response to disaster. In the 2008 general assembly, we voted to accept them as another chapter.

Right now we're working on the Panhandle because that area is very close to Tallahassee, the state capital. We always send people to Tallahassee from all over the state to educate the politicians about the issues affecting our communities. In the last few years, we had to deal with the efforts of the people and institutions looking to change laws to take away more rights from the immigrants. That convinced us that we needed to look at forming a committee there.

That's pretty much how the FWAF has grown—because of disaster and there is no response or because of needs of the community. We help the community get organized, denounce injustice, and push for response to those who should respond to the needs.

In certain industries, people make decisions on what is more profitable or what is more effective. For us, it is "How do we feel?"

As for financing our operations, most of the funds come through progressive foundations, individual funders, and program resources that support the community. I think in Florida what we have done, it's a good model of building collaboration between communities. We built a united front and a group of farmworker leaders that support each other and not compete with each other. We are one nonprofit. We get a penny, we share it with the other people. If we would have had seven organizations, we probably would have been competing with each other. We have got a good, respectful relationship. We can move people from different communities in a united way around something that will benefit all of us. We became models for others to organize.

One of our practices is that we recognize that one organization cannot solve the problems of all farmworkers. We are all needed. Whatever other organizations do, if they are good and well-intentioned, it has helped.

My feeling in the last forty years or so about how the farmworkers have been treated is that every effort by farmworkers to stay in agriculture while looking for improvements for themselves and to be better human beings has been stopped. Every institution will stop you, discourage you, tell you that you're not going to make it.

The corporate businesses or corporate farms want us to stay farmworkers for their benefit. They do not want us to become farmers. They know we are good and do not want us as competitors. If it's going to serve the industry, like if you want to become a crew leader to control the people to do what is good for the other side, you are accepted. That's why a lot of people move out of agriculture.

I say loudly, "Farmworkers are landless farmers."

We believe that the farmworkers themselves should have the right to make decisions to come up with solutions to solve their problems.

I mean, if people have the problems, they know what would change things for them. They should be part of the decision making. Most of the time when decisions have been made, other interests go first and ours go to the bottom of the pile. We want to build a better future, and the employers think we are not rational.

The farmworkers hear some of the growers talking. They say we are not human. We're like animals. We don't think and we don't react. The farmwork, I feel it is not even considered a job. And that is pretty bad. Farmworkers are hardworking people and they want to defend themselves, but how are you going to defend yourself if you don't have the tools?

The industry is very powerful. We don't have the possibilities they have. Growers have lobbyists to defend their interests in Tallahassee and nationwide. I believe the industries spend more money trying to disorganize the workers and keep them away from getting organized than what they pay them for the labor.

We don't have the money to pay what they pay to have this. We depend on volunteers to give us information on what is happening in the state house and to give us advice what legislators to talk to. Besides, the workers have been excluded from the laws that have been made for other workers. Farmworkers are prevented from forming unions.[4] We were not included in the right to know what chemicals are used in the workplace. We were instrumental to have that law changed in 1995. Now we have the Workers Protection Standard. The problem is that before '95, they exposed us and our families to all kinds of poisons that were legally permitted.[5] The growers were allowed to put farmworkers any place they needed to put them whether it was dangerous or not. They knew it was poisonous. They care more about their crops and their profits than they do the people. It's legal to make business to make money. As for people, if the law doesn't protect you, the law doesn't protect you.

Working conditions are still bad. They haven't improved that much. I mean, we've got regulations, and we've got improved sanitation in the fields, but it's still a problem.

It's a class problem. It's social injustice.

13 *The Memorial Quilts*

In January 2013, on the day Barack Obama took the oath of office for his second term, I rode on a float in the Martin Luther King Jr. Day parade. My job was to steady the aluminum pole that displayed one of the quilts hand-stitched in the memory of farmworkers who had passed away from working on the muck. We were group number fifty-nine, with half a dozen floats behind us. Ahead of us Martin Luther King Jr.'s voice blared from a loudspeaker, "I have a dream that one day . . . little black boys and black girls will be able to join hands with little white boys and little white girls as sisters and brothers."

When Jeannie Economos of the Farmworker Association of Florida invited me to participate in the parade, I hesitated. I hadn't been involved in the making of the quilts nor had I ever worked on a farm.

Half a mile into the parade, I realized the significance of my presence. The entire route was through South Apopka—or Soulville, as William Gladden called it. I, a white person, had crossed the line that had once separated the races. I was one of only a handful of Caucasians in or watching the parade.

Hundreds and hundreds of African Americans cheered from dirt-packed front yards and clapped from lawn chairs set up in front of four-room houses with rusty tin roofs. They echoed Martin Luther King Jr.'s voice, "I have a dream."

More than once I saw a woman grab the arm of a companion, point at our float, and exclaim, "There's the quilt! See my square! It's the one that . . ."

Two women, at different places along the route, called out to me. "Dale! When is the book coming out?"

I felt a humble pride to be accepted into this community, to be their messenger to the world, to be allowed to touch the fabric of the sacred object that represented so many lives.

Linda Lee stood on the opposite side of the float, proudly steadying the second quilt. She was, after all, the lead in the Quilt Project. While only two people recognized me, it seemed everyone knew Linda and called out to her by name.

Months before, Linda explained to me how she became involved in the Quilt Project:

> When they first decided they were going to do a memory quilt, it was all talk but nobody was actually getting together. Then, in 2006, my sister Margie died of a heart attack. That broke my heart. After she passed, I got real sick for over a year. It was the gallbladder. I said, "Lord, if you let me get through this, then I'm going to do whatever they decide to do about the quilt."

The project began slowly, with much discussion as to what former farmworkers could do to memorialize their friends and relatives. After they learned of a quilt that had been sewn in memory of AIDS victims, they agreed that was the perfect medium to express their feelings. Now those who had worked for others for so long expressed their distinctive creative sides.

Even after the decision was made, there were many fits and starts. Sam Chillaron, a summer intern at FWAF, interviewed Linda Lee for a college thesis. She mentioned the quilt idea, and even though he had no sewing experience, he scrounged some fabric and a needle and mocked up a sample of what a quilt square might look like. Linda Lee took one look at it and said, "Yeah, you got it." Then he went back to school and the momentum died down.

Sarah Downs came on board as a volunteer shortly after Sam left. When she learned of the quilt idea, she contacted Jim Berry, a former colleague from Michigan with experience as a museum curator and an education programmer. They talked about taking their skills in storytelling in a museum setting and putting them to work in organizing the quilt project.

They worked with FWAF to write and submit a grant application to the Florida Humanities Council. The council awarded them a minigrant, which became the seed money for the project. Jim flew in from Michigan, a community meeting was called, and FWAF bought construction paper, markers, scissors, staplers, and glue.

Jim explained how a story circle works—they went around the room and each person stated the name of the loved one they wanted to commemorate and then talked a little about him or her. After that, they cut out the shape of corn stalks or traced their hands or colored an apron or glued on figures of people fishing, cooking, and tending children. They stapled their rough designs onto a square piece of construction paper, and many of these designs later morphed into quilt squares.

The next day, the team drove 147 miles south to Indiantown. There they met with farmworkers who relocated to another farming community after the Lake Apopka farms closed. With more construction paper, markers, scissors, staplers, and glue, this group of former farmworkers tried their hands at mocking up quilt squares.

Mr. Berry filmed these two meetings and others that followed. Over a three-year period, he produced a thirty-minute documentary about the quilts titled *After the Last Harvest*.

Shortly thereafter, the Crealde School of Art in Winter Park, Florida, hosted Lauren Austin, an African American fiber artist living in Shanghai, China.[1] She created fabric art portraits and scenes on women's rights, slavery, relationships, race, and political issues. Nearly a dozen representatives from FWAF attended. All left in awe of the magnificence of what they had witnessed. This proved to be the catalyst that propelled the project into high gear.

The event expanded their understanding of what a quilt could be. A quilt could be three-dimensional. They could sew on beads, or glue on gum wrappers, or puff out an apron to stick in tiny crafted ears of corn.

Linda's only experience sewing before this time was making doll clothes, which she learned from her grandmother. After the trip to the Crealde School of Art, something came alive in Linda.

She spread out a piece of fabric and prayed. "Lord Jesus, I want to

The author in the
Martin Luther King
Jr. Day parade.
Photo by Sandra
Doran.

remember my people but I don't want it to be any kind of way. I want
to do something decent because we've always been respectful of people and do things the best we knew how. How am I going to put this
together?"

One night when she was in bed, a thought came to her. She jumped
up, grabbed a piece of paper, and wrote down her thought. The next
morning, she sketched it out.

Her grandson Michael walked in and asked, "Mama, what you doin'?"

She said, "I don't know what I'm doing, but I'm set to do it."

She designed the first quilt square for her daddy and the second one
for her mama. Linda studied her handiwork and said, "Yeah, this is
what's supposed to happen."

Late one night after Linda had worked all day on quilt squares and
was still stitching, Michael came into the room and said, "Grandma,
you need to go to bed."

Linda chuckled when she told me her reply. "Michael, shut up and
leave me alone."

Sarah and Linda tried to organize a quilting bee, but it was difficult
to coordinate schedules, so they took to visiting homes and listening to
stories. Some individuals were able to sew their own squares. For those
who could not, Linda would spend a week translating the stories into
quilt squares and then return to present the design for approval.

Some of these home visits created stories in and of themselves, including one in which an argument between a former farmworker and
some relatives resulted in the discharge of a gun. This did not deter

The Blue Quilt. All quilt photographs by Gaye Kozanli.

Sarah and Linda. They doggedly carried on their mission, cajoling each other with the words "It was more than we bargained for, but all for the cause."

After hundreds of hours of stitching, the group completed not only one quilt, their goal, but two—the Blue Quilt and the Red Quilt. Each square commemorates a specific person who worked long days with short breaks amid poisonous pesticides in humid heat or driving rain while dodging snakes and rats and biting insects—and then passed away. They also depict a people that is strong, resilient, and hopeful. The sixty squares do not come close to representing the hundreds of farmworkers who died from working on the muck.

Since that time, the quilts have been displayed in the Orlando Public Library, in the Orlando City Hall, Gainesville Public Library, at several law school environmental justice conferences, at universities, at high schools, at churches, at festivals, at fairs, and in three Martin Luther King Jr. Day parades.

The day I rode in the parade, we hung the quilts from their stands at the Farmworker Association office and loaded them onto the float pulled by a pickup truck.

I climbed onto the float and clung to a rickety rail for the four miles to the starting point. With my other hand, I clutched one of the flapping quilts, not wanting it to sustain even a stitch of damage. Sixty-four squares tell sixty-four stories. I vowed to keep their legacy alive.

Top left: Viola Robinson began working on the farms as a teenager and later married a coworker. She raised a family of three and loved to cook.

Top right: The family members of Mattie Miller Parks worked for over ten years on the muck farms. Her brother was survived by six children and her sister by two girls. Mattie passed away from cancer during the writing of this book.

Bottom left: Mary Ann Robinson created this square in memory of her mother, Annie Mae Coleman. Like many female farmworkers, Ms. Coleman wore a dress over her pants to provide privacy when "relieving herself" in the fields.

Bottom right: Jonas Ray loved to fish in Lake Apopka when not working in the muck. His sister, Magaline Duncan, remembers him as a very outgoing person—he never met a stranger.

Top left: John Raymond Cunningham worked on the muck during the 1970s. He is honored by his father in this square, which shows the crops he worked with during his years on the farm.

Top right: Juanita Gilchrist dedicated this square to the memory of her great-grandfather, M. F. Gonis, who worked on the muck farms most of his life.

Bottom left: Anna Cuevas, a lifelong farmworker, dedicated this square to her daughter who died young. Anna worked while pregnant with her daughter, who was born with tumors.

Bottom right: Geraldine Moore began working on the farms in the 1950s and hoed and packed vegetables for more than twenty years. Her sister, Linda Lee, recalls her funny jokes and love of playing cards.

Top left: Mae Eunis Phillips worked on the muck farms hoeing, packing, and cleaning the fields. She managed to complete a cosmetology degree while raising eight children.

Top right: Linda Lee dedicated this square to her cousin, Frederick Robinson, who fought in Vietnam and worked on the muck pulling weeds. He passed away as a result of being exposed to Agent Orange.

Bottom left: Louise Hamilton used this quilt square to honor the memory of her sister Betty Wright, who is depicted here in full muck garb, including gloves, an apron, pants, and boots.

Bottom right: Kenneth Smith honors his friend Jimmy in this piece that features the "Wild Cat Club" and a depiction of Jimmy with a girlfriend. Jimmy hauled corn until dying of a heart attack at the age of fifty-nine.

Top left: This square is made in memory of Johnny Jones, who loved to grill for his family of nineteen children.

Top right: Margie-Lee Pitter loved to cook various recipes when she was not running crews on the muck. The picture shows her working in the carrot house.

Bottom left: Gertrude Duval worked on the farm more than fifteen years before earning her teaching degree.

Bottom right: Henry Lee Jackson was a seasonal worker across the United States, spending the fall, winter, and spring in Apopka. He passed away from heart failure.

Top left: Magaline Duncan's brother, Jimmy Lee, worked hard on the muck all of his life picking corn. Wearing long-sleeved shirts and jeans was imperative to limit pesticide exposure.

Top right: Alice Mae Schofield ran a crew on the muck farms and loved to barbecue with family.

Bottom left: The images in this square—leafy greens, clothes, and a tractor—tell a story of chronic pesticide exposure. Tractors sprayed the chemicals on the crops that the farmworkers handled, and because spraying was often done while workers were in the fields, they took the poisons home to their families on their clothes.

Bottom right: This square honors the mothers on the muck, who dedicated themselves to raising their children while, at the same time, working to pick and process foods that fed America.

Top left: Magaline Duncan made this square in memory of her brother, Johnny Jones, who worked on the muck. She remembers how much he loved to fish and joke around with his family and friends.

Top right: Alan Dowling, brother of Johnnie Mae Dowling, picked watermelon and corn on Lake Apopka. He passed away from cancer.

Bottom left: Linda Lee dedicated this square to her grandfather, Alfred Robinson, who began working on the muck in the 1940s. He passed away as a result of lung cancer in 1963.

Bottom right: Jackie Turner began working on the farms in the 1960s as a child with her parents. She logged more than twenty years on the muck before raising her own family of four girls.

Top left: Amanda Swift dedicated this square to her aunt, Esther Banks, who was raised on a Georgia farm but spent most of her life working on the muck. She died from severe gout.

Top right: James Lee, father to Linda Lee, loved fishing and hunting and became an avid gardener after working on the muck farms for more than thirty years. He was survived by his eight children.

Bottom left: Farmworkers worked rain or shine in steep fields of mud. The farmworker in this square is wearing heavy rain gear to prevent sickness, which could mean time off work without pay.

Bottom right: Douglas Harris worked on the muck most of his life picking cabbages. Magaline Duncan, his older sister, remembers that he was a proud father of three girls and always worked hard.

Top left: Pedro Baez pays tribute to all the farmworkers who dedicated their lives to working the land and feeding America. The farmworker in this square is enjoying moments of shade after hot hours in the sun.

Top right: Earma Peterson created this square in memory of her mother and aunt. It depicts a store farmworkers frequented before work and a truck that transported more than sixty farmworkers to the farms.

Bottom left: Jonnie Mae Byars dedicated this square to her father, John Phillips, who worked in the orange groves and muck farms of Apopka.

Bottom right: Pedro Pizarro drove a tractor for the Coca-Cola grove division before dying at the age of forty-five. His clothing, like that of many farmworkers, trapped pesticide residue that was then spread to his household.

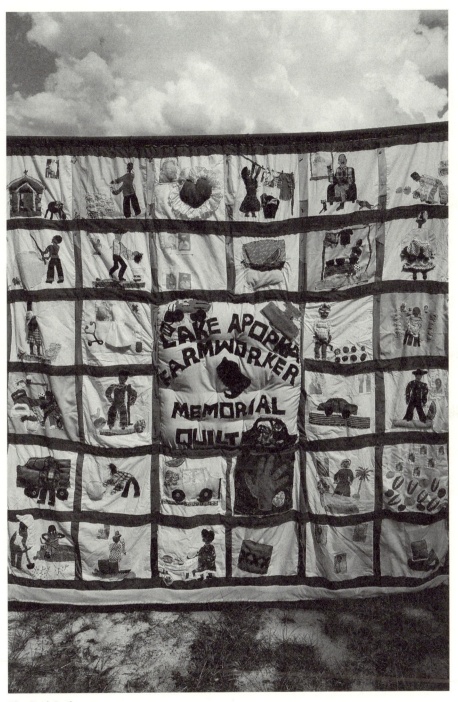

The Red Quilt.

Top left: Areatha Britten dedicated this square to her husband, Joseph, whom she described as "always working." He loved to volunteer at their church when he was not in the fields of Lake Apopka.

Top right: Daniel Dawson worked on the muck as a seasonal worker and is pictured in this square stacking boxes of corn.

Bottom left: Amanda Robinson-Lee, mother to principal quilt-maker Linda Lee, loved to cook and care for her large family of eight kids. She worked on the muck farms for twenty-five years.

Bottom right: Aaron Harris was hearing impaired, but that did not prevent him from working on the muck. He is pictured here fishing, one of the pastimes most remembered of Apopka men.

Top left: Alberta Jones, mother of Magaline Duncan, worked on the muck with her children for fifteen years. The square shows her hanging clothes for her nineteen kids.

Top right: John H. Dubose worked on the muck for twenty-two years. He died one year later from cancer, leaving thirteen kids and a wife. He is pictured here with his favorite things: tea, a detective novel, and a turtle for turtle soup. He did not like his cat.

Bottom left: Magaline Duncan made this square in memory of her brother, James William Dawson, who worked on the muck most of his life. Magaline remembers him as a "nutty guy."

Bottom right: Willy V. Robinson taught all of his nieces softball when he was not on a tractor for the farms or spraying pesticides. He passed away as a result of throat cancer.

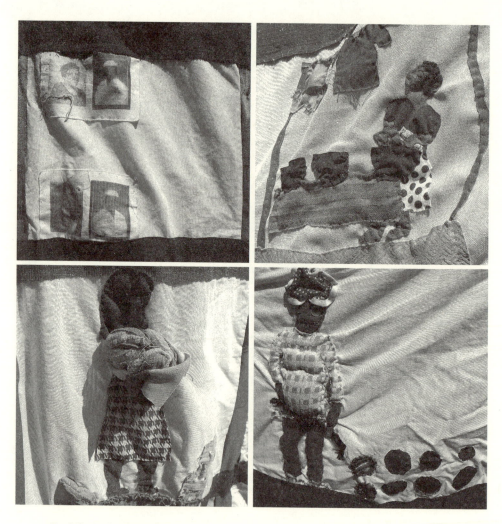

Top left: Arphia Graves uses the last remaining pictures of her family members to tell their story of loss. Annie Green and Richard Graves Mims worked on the muck for over twenty years.

Top right: This square is made in memory of Magaline Duncan's niece, Emily Burdon, who worked on the muck for five to six years. She is pictured in the square hanging clothes for her four kids.

Bottom left: Joyce Ann Burdon worked on the muck picking corn with her sister Magaline.

Bottom right: Mary Tinsley made this square in honor of the moms who worked in the fields with their children. The square depicts Mary's mother pregnant with her and her twin sister. Mary now works with the Florida Lupus Foundation.

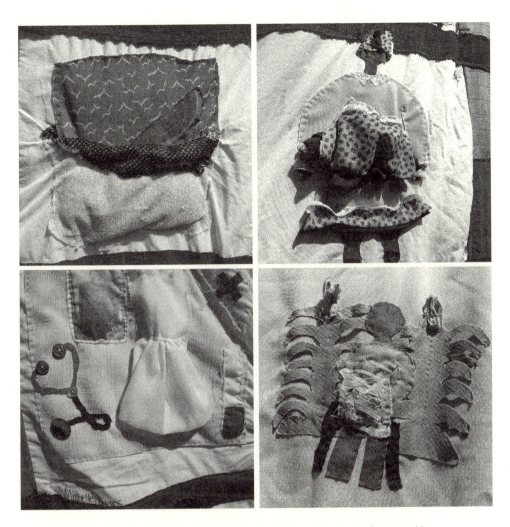

Top left: This square represents the birds that flew over the muck farms and later died as a result of their exposure to pesticides in one of the largest inland mass bird deaths in history. Farmworkers' health was never studied to link their ailments to pesticides.

Top right: Vivian Bimbo worked on the farms while also raising eight children, who all did hard labor with her and their father. She died of kidney failure.

Bottom left: Michelle Byars, daughter of Jonnie Mae Byars, studied to become a nurse after working on the muck. Unfortunately, she died before completing her degree.

Bottom right: Nadie Sue of Indiantown created this square in memory of her son, pictured here packing corn on the muck.

Top left: Heraldean Turner organized garage sales for the community when she did not work on the muck.

Top right: Emma and J. W. Mallory both passed away from cancer after working on the muck for twenty years. The car/road image is significant for the husband and wife duo, who traveled north during the off-season for migrant work.

Bottom left: James Alfred Lee drove vegetables for the Apopka muck farms and later owned his own fleet of trucks for over ten years. He was the beloved brother of Linda Lee.

Bottom right: "Baby" Ray Lee worked on the muck farms during the 1950s as a truck loader until leaving to work for an electric company.

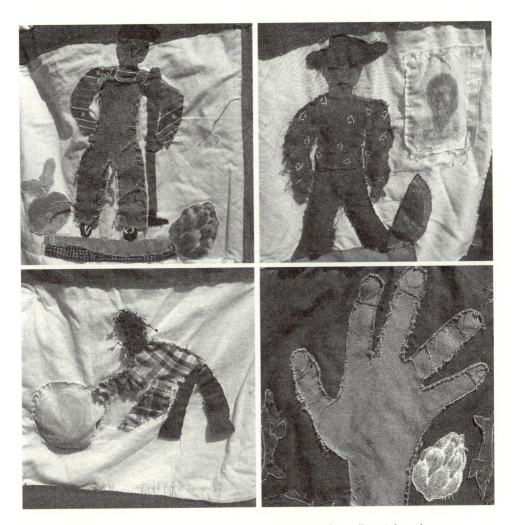

Top left: Richard Robinson is remembered by family as a fast-talking joker who ran a crew on the farms.

Top right: Willie V. Robinson Jr. passed away from stomach cancer after working in farms and nurseries.

Bottom left: Johnnin-May Dowling of Indiantown dedicated this square to Aaron Taylor, who worked on the farms spraying pesticide for most of his life. He died of cancer at the age of forty.

Bottom right: Marshall Smith worked on the muck for thirty-five years. After spraying pesticides, Marshall became ill and died. The hand is marked with red scratches, the result of packing corn.

Top left: Earlene Wallace was known by family as a tall tale teller. She worked on the farms for more than ten years and spent the last years of her life working in a nursing home in Altamonte Springs, Florida.

Top right: John Johnson, uncle of Earma Peterson, took such pride in farming that he worked his own garden of peanuts at home after long hours on the muck. His wife, Lula, loved playing with cats on their porch.

Bottom left: Willie Mae Davis worked in the carrot house for more than ten years. She loved to bake foods like these fancy cakes. Ms. Davis died of a heart attack.

Bottom right: Albert Lee and Alfred Parks are honored by their mother, Mattie Miller Parks. Albert was survived by seven children, and Alfred was survived by two children.

Top left: Louise Hamilton honors her mother, Beatrice Wright, in this square that portrays her mother busily picking the crops of Lake Apopka. Her mother worked on the farms for thirty years to support her family.

Top right: Jessie Mae Jefferson Robinson died at the age of seventy-six, having survived more than fifty years on the muck. She is pictured having lunch on a discarded DDT container, unaware of its harmful residue. Regulations did not exist to prevent this casual exposure.

Bottom left: This square represents the pesticides sprayed in the fields, sometimes directly onto the muck workers as they tended to the crops. The direct exposure caused intergenerational health issues, often affecting farmworkers' grandchildren.

Bottom right: One of the quilt project's main intentions is to raise awareness about the harmful effects of pesticide exposure, which is still too often unregulated. This square honors all farmworkers, unmentioned by name but not forgotten.

Epilogue

View from the South Side

I had spent so much time on the north shore of Lake Apopka, where the farmlands had once been and the former farmworkers live, that I decided to visit the south side to meditate upon all I had learned over the four years I'd spent writing this book. I drove twenty miles to a nature preserve that was developed by a citizens' action group in response to the Lake Apopka Restoration Project. I parked my car in the dirt lot between two silver convertibles and walked along a boardwalk through junglelike terrain.

Spanish moss engulfed bushes like giant spider webs and dangled from tree branches like limp witch's hair. I passed an enormous tree that had fallen to reveal the private underbelly of its root system. Every few yards or so signs identified the plants and trees growing under, around, and over the boardwalk—swamp dogwood, pickerelweed, downy maiden fern, cabbage palm, bandana of the Everglades, saltmarsh mallow. The shades of green ranged from olive to lime to Christmas tree to forest to hues I could not describe.

I walked at a fast clip until I came to a pavilion overlooking Lake Apopka. A white film rippled around the water hibiscus growing along the edge of the lake. Two great blue herons took to the air and flew in unison not far from where I sat. One squawked like something you'd hear in Jurassic Park. Quiet and peaceful, this appeared to be a place to commune with nature. A place to rejuvenate.

The author writing in the Oakland Preserve.

I peered across the choppy green waters, barely able to make out the shoreline on the north side. Over there, I had visited the homes of many African American former farmworkers—homes without screens or air conditioning; homes with blue tarps covering roofs in need of repair; homes with families living on the edge; homes whose occupants had seen too many funerals. The south side is all about distance from the past, about looking ahead, about curb appeal.

This was only the third time I had visited the south shore. The first time was for a program titled "5,000 Years of History of Lake Apopka." It was held in a brand-new community center overlooking Lake Apopka. "Take Me Home, Country Roads" set the upbeat tone as I entered the room. Nearly a hundred people chatted amicably before taking seats in padded chairs. All attendees were white.

I sat through the program remembering my interviews with African Americans whose families, a century ago, had walked or paddled hundreds of miles to work on farms, and I waited for their stories to be told. In fact, farmworkers on the north shore were skipped altogether in the historical storytelling. We learned of the Seminole Indians, of the 1842 settling of the land by whites, of the 1845 Indian Removal Committee, of the beginning of citrus farming in 1870, of the fish camps and the building of the canal, of the algae bloom and the bird deaths. Oh yes, I almost forgot: African Americans *were* mentioned. In 1822, I believe it was, one white man arrived with two slaves.

Sitting in the pavilion, I watched a white egret rise from the eelgrass, hover over the lake, and fight the wind to stay in one place, peering into the water for fish. For a moment, I spotted the black, snakelike neck of an anhinga bobbing above the water; it plunged under and resurfaced again ten feet away. I spied a brick mansion through a cutout of trees one-quarter of the way up the left side of the lake. It was part of one of the new communities, with homes valued at over $1 million and golf courses and spa amenities, marketed to clueless out-of-towners as "beautiful lakeside property."

I can't help but wonder whether they know that the contaminated muck at the bottom of the lake is twenty-five feet thick in places.[1]

The second time I came to the south end of the lake was for the First Annual Lake Apopka Restoration Summit. State senators and representatives, scientists and planners of water management districts, senior staff of environmental agencies, academics, and friends of the lake gathered to report on what they had accomplished over the previous fifteen years and to discuss the future. It was too abstract for me. I took fourteen pages of notes, but at one point I became so overwhelmed with the technical language that I opened a game of solitaire on my iPad. Within seconds, an armed sheriff squatted by my side. "That isn't very nice, ma'am," he said, so I put it away.

Nonetheless, my notes include words like limnology, cultural eutrophication, feasibility studies, alum treatment, flocculation, hydraulic dredging, biomanipulation, and a lot about phosphorous load. Reduction of phosphorous load, it seems, is the biggest goal.

As for remediation of the land, a plan called "soil inversion" has been put into place. Organochlorine pesticides remain in the soil; however, a modified farm plow has flipped over the top 30 centimeters of soil on certain sections of the former farmlands.[2]

I recently walked on that land on the north shore, which the Audubon Society lists as one of the most important "hot spots" for migratory birds and resident species anywhere in North America. The December 2012 Christmas Bird Count listed sightings of over 350 species.[3] A sign at the entrance reads, "Warning: Visitors must stay on road. No fishing is allowed on this property. These lands are former agricultural lands that were subjected to regular use of agricultural chemicals, some of which, such as DDT, are persistent in the environment and may present a risk to human health."

This, fifteen years after the last farmworker left the fields; this, after the top layer of soil has been buried.

My feelings were mixed as I sat in the quiet pavilion. People on either side of the lake probably don't think much about the other side, nor do many of them know that the issue of pesticide poisoning in and around Lake Apopka is now of global concern.

Pesticide Action Network (PAN) International conducted a four-year investigation, in which they identified and worked with communities around the world whose health and environment were compromised and damaged due to the use of highly poisonous chemical pesticides. They brought representatives from these communities to testify before the Permanent People's Tribunal (PPT),[4] an international people's court that considers charges in cases of massive human rights violations, through which people, communities, and organizations can seek some sense of validation for their claims when they feel justice has not been served by national or international courts or any other means.[5] The Lake Apopka farmworker community was one of twenty-five communities listed as plaintiffs in the case against the six largest transnational pesticide companies around the globe.

I chuckle when I remember the trial. It took place December 3–6, 2011, in Bangalore, India, and was broadcast live. I set my alarm for 3 a.m. and, across town, so did my daughter, Karen. We logged into the broadcast and messaged one another. I thought there was something wrong with my volume until Karen told me she couldn't hear either. I tweeted the PAN representative in Bangalore that there was no sound, and he tweeted back that they were trying to fix the problem. The first thing I heard when the volume was restored was the line, "Someone tweeted they couldn't hear." Halfway across the world, I knew they were talking about me.

I waited eagerly for the PPT to release their verdict against the six companies who manufactured the pesticides. In March 2012, they published a 274-page report stating that highly toxic pesticides are produced, marketed, and used, and that the result is great suffering that largely affects "small farmers, farm laborers, the poor and powerless."[6]

Regarding the Lake Apopka farmworkers, the PPT wrote that "the African-American Lake Apopka farmworker community is an aging community that in many cases had parents, grandparents, children and grandchildren working alongside each other in the fields. Hence, the bioaccumulative properties of these pesticides have negatively impacted multiple generations of farmworkers with long-term, chronic health problems from cumulative and synergistic effects."[7]

And they spoke the words that have been so long in coming: "The case of the Lake Apopka farmworkers calls for justice. They offered their labour planting and harvesting and packing crops to grow food for the country, all the while unknowingly burdening their bodies forever with poisons."[8]

A month later, in April 2012, a PAN representative hand-delivered a letter to a top White House environmental official urging the Obama administration to address the need for accountability in these cases of pesticide poisonings and environmental impacts.

So here we sit now—those whose maladies hold them hostage to the past, those looking toward the future who want to forget the past, and those of us who wonder what was learned from the past so that it will never be repeated.

Appendix

What You Can Do to Make a Difference

People and organizations around the world believe that food should be not only locally grown, organic, and sustainable but also fair and just to the workers who produce it. You can help make a difference by learning more about these groups. The problems Lake Apopka farmworkers have experienced with pesticides are not unique. Many of these organizations raise similar concerns.

Farmworker Association of Florida (FWAF)

http://www.floridafarmworkers.org
The Farmworker Association of Florida is a membership organization of eight thousand farmworker families. The association addresses farmworkers' wages, benefits, and working conditions as well as pesticides, field sanitation, disaster response, immigration, and other community-based issues.

FWAF Memorial Quilt

The memorial quilt is a project of the Farmworker Association. Each square depicts an individual who worked on the farms and has since passed away. The quilt has been on display in many locations.
http://apopkaquiltproject.blogspot.com

Farmworker Health and Safety Institute

http://www.cata-farmworkers.org
The Farmworker Health and Safety Institute is a consortium of three community-based farmworker organizations that work with farmworkers along the Eastern Migrant Stream and the U.S.–Mexico border and in the Caribbean. Members include El Comité de Apoyo a los Trabajadores Agrícolas (CATA), the Farmworker Association of Florida, and the Border Agricultural Workers Project (BAWP). CATA and FWAF formed the institute in 1992 in order to work together on a regional level to protect the health and safety of farmworkers against environmental hazards such as pesticides.

Organizations in Which the Farmworker Association of Florida Is Involved

Agricultural Justice Project

http://www.agriculturaljusticeproject.org
The Agricultural Justice Project works to ensure respectful treatment for all food system workers and fair prices to farmers that cover the costs of production, the protection of children from hazardous farmwork, and living wages.

Domestic Fair Trade Association

http://www.thedfta.org
The mission of DFTA is to promote and protect the integrity of domestic fair trade principles and practices through education, marketing, advocacy, and endorsement.

Farmworker Justice

http://www.farmworkerjustice.org
Farmworker Justice is a nonprofit organization that seeks to empower migrant and seasonal farmworkers to improve their living and working conditions, immigration status, health, occupational safety, and access to justice.

Food Chain Workers Alliance

http://www.foodchainworkers.org
The Food Chain Workers Alliance works to build a more sustainable food system that respects workers' rights, based on the principles of social,

environmental, and racial justice, in which everyone has access to healthy and affordable food.

Hope CommUnity Center

http://hcc-offm.org
The Hope CommUnity Center, formerly known as the Office for Farmworker Ministry, is a community-based organization founded in 1971. Over the years, the ministry has fostered the development of many self-help, community, and worker organizations to meet basic human needs. The center is a visible sign of the ministry's continued welcoming presence and is a home for bringing together diverse peoples and cultures working for peace in the community and the world.

La Via Campesina

http://www.viacampesina.org
La Via Campesina brings together organizations of peasants, family farmers, indigenous peoples, farmworkers, women, and rural youth from some seventy countries worldwide, representing about five hundred million families of women and men of the land.

National Farm Worker Ministry

http://nfwm.org
National Farm Worker Ministry is a faith-based organization that supports farmworkers as they organize for justice and empowerment.

Pesticide Action Network of North America

http://www.panna.org
Pesticide Action Network of North America is an organization seeking healthier alternatives to pesticides in day-to-day life and taking collective action to create real change.

Student Action with Farmworkers

http://saf-unite.org
Student Action with Farmworkers is a 501(c)3 nonprofit organization whose mission is to bring students and farmworkers together to learn about each other's lives, share resources and skills, improve conditions for farmworkers, and build diverse coalitions working for social change.

U.S. Food Sovereignty Alliance

http://www.usfoodsovereigntyalliance.org
The U.S. Food Sovereignty Alliance believes that food and water must be treated as basic human rights, and they uphold the internationally recognized principles of food sovereignty. They honor Mother Earth, value biodiversity, and support ecological farming and fishing practices that protect the earth, animals, and people.

They support movement away from the dominant corporate-controlled food system, which is shaped by systems of power and oppression. They believe solutions must dismantle systemic food injustice rooted in race, class, and gender oppression.

They respect people and other forms of life over profits. They honor everyone's work in the food system, including unpaid, underpaid, and devalued labor. They work to honor our human commonalities and restore traditional ways of growing, preparing, sharing, and eating food as a community.

Other Pesticide and Farmworker Organizations

Beyond Pesticides, http://www.beyondpesticides.org
Border Agricultural Workers Project, http://www.farmworkers.org/
    bawppage.html
Centro Campesino, http://www.centrocampesino.org
California Rural Legal Assistance, Inc., http://www.crla.org
Coalition of Immokalee Workers, http://www.ciw-online.org
Farm Labor Organizing Committee, http://www.supportfloc.org
Pineros Campesinos Unides Noroeste, http://www.pcun.org
United Farm Workers, http://www.ufw.org

Glossary

agrochemical. A chemical, such as a pesticide, used for agricultural purposes.

algae bloom. The rapid and excessive growth of algae generally caused by high nutrient levels combined with other conditions favorable to plant life. Blooms can deoxygenate the water, leading to the death of wildlife.

autoimmune disease. A disease in which the immune system cannot tell the difference between foreign invaders and the body's healthy tissues and creates autoantibodies that attack and destroy healthy tissue. These autoantibodies cause inflammation, pain, and damage in various parts of the body.

bioaccumulation. The accumulation of a substance, such as a toxic chemical, in the tissues of a living organism.

blackjack. A short, leather-covered club, used as a weapon, consisting of a heavy head on a flexible handle.

chlordane. A chlorinated hydrocarbon used as an insecticide that can be absorbed through the skin with resultant severe toxic effects.

contractor. An individual who contracts with farm owners to supply farmworkers to plant, harvest, and pack the produce. They oversee the transportation of seasonal employees to the farms and the camps in which the farmworkers live.

crew leader. An individual who supervises a labor crew in the field, acting as an intermediary between farm owners and the workers. May also be a contractor.

effluent. Sewage, both treated and untreated.

endocrine disruptors. Chemicals that interfere with the body's endocrine system and produce adverse developmental, reproductive, neurological, and immunological effects in humans and wildlife.

environmental justice. The fair treatment and meaningful involvement of all people regardless of race, color, national origin, or income with respect to the development, implementation, and enforcement of environmental laws, regulations, and policies.

Farmworker Association of Florida. A statewide organization of eight thousand members committed to organizing farmworkers more effectively in their struggle for better housing, wages, and working conditions. They have been instrumental in the passing of laws and educating farmworkers regarding hazardous chemicals.

fernery. A greenhouse specializing in the growing of ferns.

H-2A visa. A temporary work visa acquired through a program that allows agricultural employers to hire workers from other countries to fill agricultural jobs that last ten months or less. To bring in H-2A guest workers, employers must first show that they have tried and are unable to find U.S. workers to meet their labor needs. Although the H-2A program includes some basic requirements to protect U.S. workers from negative effects on their wages and working conditions and protect foreign workers from exploitation, it has been criticized for failing to protect vulnerable workers.

hamper. A wide-mouthed container of basketwork that may be carried on the back during the harvesting of fruit or vegetables by workers in the field. The contents of the hamper may be emptied regularly into larger containers or a cart, wagon, or truck.

insecticide. A pesticide that kills insects.

Intracoastal Waterway. A three-thousand-mile waterway along the Atlantic and Gulf coasts of the United States that provides a navigable route along its length without many of the hazards of travel on the open sea.

juke. A roadside drinking establishment that offers cheap drinks, food, and music for dancing.

lupus. An autoimmune disease that can damage any part of the body (skin, joints, and/or internal organs). Symptoms may ebb and flow so that patients may feel good sometimes and be incapacitated at other times.

muck. A highly organic dark or black soil. As used in this book, the fertile soil in and along the edges of Lake Apopka.

mule train. A large piece of farm equipment used in the harvesting of vegetables. Wings extend from each side. As many as seven farmworkers per side walk below it, picking vegetables and tossing them up to others, who are riding on the mule train and pack the harvest into boxes.

organochlorine pesticide. Chlorinated hydrocarbons used extensively from the 1940s through the 1960s in agriculture and mosquito control. Many have since been banned in the United States, although a few are still registered for use. Exposure to organochlorine pesticides can occur through inhalation as well as ingestion of fish, dairy products, and other fatty foods that are contaminated. Organochlorine pesticides accumulate in the environment. They are very persistent and move long distances in surface runoff or groundwater. Exposure to organochlorine pesticides over a short period may produce convulsions, headache, dizziness, nausea, vomiting, tremors, confusion, muscle weakness, slurred speech, salivation, and sweating. Long-term exposure to organochlorine pesticides can damage the liver, kidney, central nervous system, thyroid, and bladder.

Paragon. A pesticide company. Many farmworkers refer to chemicals produced by the company as "Paragon."

Permanent People's Tribunal. An international opinion tribunal founded in 1979 in Italy on principles outlined in the "Universal Declaration of the Rights of Peoples," which adjudicates complaints of human rights abuses submitted by the affected communities. It uses the rigorous conventional court format and issues indictments, names relevant laws, and documents findings. While its verdicts are not legally binding, they can set precedents for future legal actions against, in the case examined in this book, agrochemical corporations.

pesticide. Any substance used to kill, repel, or control certain forms of plant or animal life considered to be pests.

Pesticide Action Network. A worldwide organization that works to replace the use of hazardous pesticides with ecologically sound and socially just alternatives.

Piccolo. See **Juke.**

persistent organic pollutants (POPS). Toxic chemicals that adversely affect human health and the environment around the world. Because they can be transported by wind and water, most POPs can and do affect people and wildlife far from where they are used and released. They persist for long periods of time in the environment and can accumulate and pass from one species to the next through food chains.

Reconstruction. The period of history in the United States following the Civil War, from 1865 to 1877, when society was adjusting to the end of slavery.

seasonal worker. A farmworker who travels between farms planting or harvesting produce based on the season.

sentinel species. A species whose presence, absence, or well-being is indicative of the environment as a whole.

sharecropper. A tenant farmer who pays rent with a share of crops instead of money.

St. Johns River Water Management District. The organization responsible for managing groundwater and surface water resources in all or part of eighteen counties in northeast and east central Florida.

synergistic. Refers to an interaction involving two or more forces in which the combined effect is greater than the sum of individual effects.

toxaphene. One of the most common pesticides in the United States in the 1970s and early 1980s. It was used primarily to control insect pests on cotton and other crops in the southern United States. Toxaphene was banned by 1990. It affects the endocrine system and liver and is categorized by the NIH as "reasonably anticipated" to be a human carcinogen.

transnational corporation. Any corporation that is registered and operates in more than one country at a time.

Acknowledgments

Thank you to the following people, who extended invaluable help and support during the writing of this book:

Jeannie Economos, pesticide health and safety project coordinator with the Farmworker Association of Florida, who has made it her mission to keep the stories of the African American former farmworkers of Lake Apopka alive. She guided me through the project, took me on a toxic tour of South Apopka, arranged for the interviews, and read many drafts of the project.

Karen Slongwhite Greene, who introduced me to the Lake Apopka farmworkers, read multiple drafts of the book, assisted in the final preparation of the manuscript, and offered guidance, encouragement, and new information.

Sarah Downs, who drove to and from Indiantown twice for our interviews and provided invaluable information on the Quilt Project.

Ann Marie Monzione of Red Moon Writing, who helped craft a query letter and submission package.

Gaye Kozanli, a photographer with a gift for capturing an individual's personality.

Geoff Benge, who designed the maps.

Sonia Dickey and Nevil Parker at the University Press of Florida, who guided me through the publishing process.

James W. Finley, my father, who passed away at the age of eighty-nine shortly after the book was accepted for publication. Many afternoons, we bought a cup of coffee at Dunkin' Donuts, drove to the quiet wooded area that used to be Mead's Bottom, and he listened as I read aloud and edited many chapters. He was enthusiastic about the project and proud of me for doing it.

David Slongwhite, my husband, who listened to hundreds of drafts and who put up with a messy house, quickly prepared meals, and my getting up to write in the middle of the night when the muse struck.

Cooper David, who assisted with the captions.

Lee David, an avid reader whose opinion I greatly value.

All the former farmworkers who opened their hearts and shared their stories.

Notes

Prologue

1. "Endocrine Disruptors," National Institute of Environmental Health Web site, last modified June 5, 2013, http://www.niehs.nih.gov/health/topics/agents/endocrine/index.cfm.

2. Farm owners are not the same as farmworkers. Farmworkers are laborers who plant, harvest, and pack the vegetables. Individuals known as farmers, farm owners, and growers own the farms. Frequently, a grower will hire an individual called a crew leader, boss man, or labor contractor to act as intermediary between themselves and the farmworkers. They manage the laborers, in some cases very harshly, and are usually the same ethnicity as the laborers. This arrangement helps farm owners avoid responsibility for the treatment of the laborers.

3. "Environmental Justice is the fair treatment and meaningful involvement of all people regardless of race, color, national origin, or income with respect to the development, implementation, and enforcement of environmental laws, regulations, and policies." Environmental Protection Agency Web site, last modified September 12, 2013, http://www.epa.gov/environmentaljustice.

4. Robert Bullard, "The Legacy of American Apartheid and Environmental Racism," *Journal of Civil Rights and Economic Development* 9, no. 2 (1994), 7–8, http://scholarship.law.stjohns.edu/jcred/vol9/iss2/3.

Chapter 1: Background of Lake Apopka

1. "Harris Chain Bass Fishing Overview," Lake County Bass Web site, accessed September 26, 2013, http://www.lakecountybass.com/harris-chain-bass-fishing-overview.html.

2. Bryan Nelson, "First Annual Lake Apopka Restoration Summit Recap," *The District 38 Update*, posted December 20, 2011, http://staterepbryannel-son.wordpress.com/2011/12/20/recap-from-the-first-annual-lake-apopka-restoration-summit.

3. Daniel Canfield Jr., Robert W. Bachmann, and Mark V. Hoyer, "A Management Alternative for Lake Apopka," *Lake and Reservoir Management* 16, no. 3 (2000): 214, http://lakewatch.ifas.ufl.edu/LWTEAMFOLDER/CanfieldPubs/ApopkaManAlt.pdf.

4. "Lake Apopka Timeline," Friends of Lake Apopka Web site, http://www.fola.org/PDFs/LakeApopkaTimelineAug2011.pdf; Canfield, Bachmann, and Hoyer, "A Management Alternative for Lake Apopka."

5. Henry F. Swanson, "History of the Vegetable Industry," in *Countdown to Agriculture in Orange County, Florida* (Orlando, Fla.: Designers Press of Orlando, 1975), 199.

6. Ibid.

7. Ibid., 200.

8. Ibid., 197.

9. Florida Senate Committee on Agriculture, "Status of Health-Related Consequences to Muck Farm Workers in the Lake Apopka Region," *Florida Senate*, issue brief 2012-2201, December 14, 2011, http://www.flsenate.gov/Published-Content/Session/2012/InterimReports/AG2012012-201ag.pdf.

10. "Lake Apopka Timeline," Friends of Lake Apopka Web site.

11. Mary Jane Angelo, "Stumbling toward Success: A Story of Adaptive Law and Ecological Resilience," *Nebraska Law Review* 87, no. 4 (2008): 966.

12. Swanson, "History of the Vegetable Industry," 220.

13. "Persistent Organic Pollutants: A Global Issue, a Global Response," Environmental Protection Agency Web site, last modified July 30, 2012, http://www.epa.gov/international/toxics/pop.html.

14. Ibid.

15. "DDT: A Brief History and Status," Environmental Protection Agency Web site, last modified May 9, 2012, http://www.epa.gov/pesticides/fact-sheets/chemicals/ddt-brief-history-status.htm.

16. Gila Neta, Lynn R. Goldman, Dana Barr, Benjamin J. Apelberg, Frank R. Witter, and Rolf U. Halden, "Fetal Exposure to Chlordane and Permethrin Mixtures in Relation to Inflammatory Cytokins and Birth Outcomes," *Environmental Science and Technology* 45, no. 4 (2011), 1680–87, http://pubs.acs.org/doi/ipdf/10.1021/es103417j.

17. "Chlordane," Environmental Protection Agency Web site, last modified November 6, 2007, http://www.epa.gov/ttn/atw/hlthef/chlordan.html.

18. William Gladden, interview with author, 2012.

19. Ibid.

20. Ibid.

21. "'Superfund' is the name given to the environmental program established to address abandoned hazardous waste sites. This law was established after the discovery of toxic waste dumps in the 1970s and allows the EPA to clean up the sites and to compel responsible parties to perform cleanups or reimburse the government for EPA-led cleanups. "Basic Information," Environmental Protection Agency Web site, last modified May 14, 2012, http://www.epa.gov/superfund/about.htm.

22. Angelo, "Stumbling toward Success," 966.

23. "Lake Apopka Timeline," Friends of Lake Apopka Web site.

24. Ibid.

25. "Environmental Contaminants and Gators," Wild Florida Ecotravel Guide, accessed September 26, 2013, http://www.wildflorida.com/wildlife/gators/Environmental_Contaminants_and_Alligators.php.

26. Christina Hernandez Sherwood, "Q & A: Louis Guillette Jr., endowed chair of Marine Genomics, Medical University of South Carolina," SmartPlanet Web site, posted October 25, 2011, http://www.smartplanet.com/blog/puregenius/q-a-louis-guillette-jr-endowed-chair-of-marine-genomics-medical-university-of-south-carolina/7265.

27. Ibid.

28. Theo Colborn is founder of the Endocrine Disruption Exchange, an international nonprofit that compiles and disseminates scientific evidence on environmental and health problems caused by low-level exposure to chemicals that interfere with development and function, called endocrine disruptors.

29. "Interviews—Louis J Guillette | Fooling With Nature | FRONTLINE | PBS," PBS Web site, accessed September 24, 2013, http://www.pbs.org/wgbh/pages/frontline/shows/nature/interviews/guillette.html.

30. "Dr. Louis Guillette Earns Prestigious Heinz Award," *Medical University of South Carolina Research News*, September 2011, http://academicdepartments.musc.edu/musc/news/res_news/sept11_guillette.htm.

31. Ibid., video link, accessed July 4, 2012.

32. "Fish Consumption and Environmental Justice: A Report Developed from the National Environmental Justice Advisory Council Meeting of December 3–6, 2001," Environmental Protection Agency Web site, http://www.epa.gov/environmentaljustice/resources/publications/nejac/fish-consump-report_1102.pdf.

33. MACTEC, "Lake Apopka North Shore Restoration Area Feasibility Study: Orange and Lake Counties, Florida," section I-5, http://www.sjrwmd.com/technicalreports/pdfs/SP/SJ2010-SP6.pdf.

34. Katherine Bouma, "Lake Apopka Bird Deaths Hit 1,000," *Orlando Sentinel*,

May 8, 1999, http://articles.orlandosentinel.com/1999-05-08/news/990507 1199_1_dead-birds-pesticides-lake-apopka.

35. Angelo, "Stumbling toward Success, 966.

36. Bouma, "Lake Apopka Bird Deaths Hit 1,000."

37. Ibid.

38. Ibid.

39. MACTEC, "Lake Apopka North Shore Restoration Area Feasibility Study."

40. "Lake Apopka Timeline," Friends of Lake Apopka Web site.

41. Ibid.

42. Lawrence Budd, "Doing a Job on the Farmworkers," *Orlando Weekly*, May 7, 1998, http://www2.orlandoweekly.com/news/story.asp?id=680.

43. Jason Garcia, "Safety Net Fails Farmworkers," *Orlando Sentinel*, October 5, 2003.

44. Ibid.

45. Eugenia Economos, interview with author, January 2012.

46. "Follow-up Healthcare Meeting," The Forgotten Farmworkers of Apopka blog, posted by "Rachel," August 27, 2007, http://apopkafarmworkers.blogspot.com/search?q=fish&max-results=20&by-date=true.

47. WESH TV News broadcast, March 26, 1999.

48. Angela Lopez, "Legislator's Plans to Help Apopka Workers Move Forward," *Florida Independent*, September 29, 2011, http://floridaindependent.com/49133/gary-siplin-farm-workers.

49. Ibid.

50. Angela Lopez, "Fla. Senator: Scott Budget Allows Poor Black Farmworkers to Die," *Florida Independent*, September 29, 2012, http://floridaindependent.com/75448/rick-scott-budget-veto-apopka-gary-siplin.

51. "Congresswoman Lee Discussing Poverty and Florida Farmworkers," YouTube video, posted by "Rep. Barbara Lee," May 1, 2012, http://www.youtube.com/watch?v=ZsohdrGMhzw.

52. "'Big 6' Guilty of Human Rights Violations," Pesticide Action Network North America Web site, December 7, 2011, http://www.panna.org/big-6/press-release/big-6-guilty-human-rights-violations.

53. "History of Lake Apopka," St. Johns River Water Management District Web site, accessed September 25, 2013, http://floridaswater.com/lakeapopka/history.html.

54. "Commissioner Wants to Spend $1M to Clean Up Lake Apopka," WFTV Web site, posted July 17, 2012, http://www.wftv.com/news/news/local/commissioner-wants-spend-1m-clean-lake-apopka/nPxCL.

55. Ibid.

56. Kevin Spear, "Can Growing Hay on Dredged Muck Ease Lake Apopka Pollution?" *Orlando Sentinel*, June 10, 2013, http://articles.orlandosentinel.com/2013-06-10/news/os-lake-apopka-controversial-cure-20130610_1_lake-apopka-50-square-mile-lake-fourth-largest-lake.

57. Stephen Hudak, "Summit Envisions Eco-tourism Future for Lake Apopka's North Shore," *Orlando Sentinel*, February 26, 2013, http://articles.orlando-sentinel.com/2013-06-10/news/os-lake-apopka-controversial-cure-20130610_1_lake-apopka-50-square-mile-lake-fourth-largest-lake.

Chapter 2: "Hard to Believe Unless You Lived through It"

1. Paragon was actually the manufacturer of the pesticide, not the product name.

2. "According to a 1945 U.S. Army report, 830 German POWs were stationed at the Orlando and Leesburg Airfields, providing manpower to several branch camps dotted around Orange, Osceola, Lake and Seminole Counties. The branch camps housed prisoners contracted by private businesses to work in fields and packing houses. West Orange County, with its vast citrus groves and vegetable farms, had a great need for labor." Jacob Flynn, "German Prisoners of War in Central Florida during the Second World War," *Heritage Windows*, Winter 2011, http://www.wghf.org/wp-content/uploads/2011/03/WGHF_Winter-2011-Newsletter.pdf.

Chapter 4: "Not Enough Cheekbones to Hold Your Tears"

1. "Methyl bromide (MeBr) is an odorless, colorless gas that has been used as a soil fumigant to control pests across a wide range of agricultural sectors. Because MeBr depletes the stratospheric ozone layer, the amount of MeBr produced and imported in the U.S. was reduced incrementally until it was phased out in January 1, 2005, pursuant to our obligations under the *Montreal Protocol on Substances that Deplete the Ozone Layer* (Protocol) and the Clean Air Act (CAA)." "The Phaseout of Methyl Bromide," Environmental Protection Agency Web site, last modified July 16, 2013, http://www.epa.gov/ozone/mbr.

2. "Methyl bromide is a dangerous cumulative poison with delayed symptoms of central nervous system intoxication that may appear as long as several months after exposure. High concentrations can produce fatal pulmonary edema. Chronic exposure can cause central nervous system depression and kidney injury. It may cause severe and permanent brain damage. Severe neurological signs may appear when there is a sudden exposure to high concentrations following continuous slight exposure. Methyl bromide has practically no odor or irritating effects and therefore no warning, even at hazardous concentrations." "Chemical Data Sheet: Methyl Bromide," National Oceanic and

Atmospheric Administration Web site, accessed September 25, 2013, http://cameochemicals.noaa.gov/chemical/1091.

Chapter 5: "God Made Up for My Lost Children"

1. "On August 18, 1887, only ten years removed from Reconstruction (1863–1877), a group of twenty-seven Negro men (led by Joe Clark) convened with the purpose of founding, what would turn out to be, the first incorporated African American settlement community in the United States." Historic Town of Eatonville Web site, accessed October 29, 2014, http://www.townofeatonville.org.

2. "Hospital/medical/infectious waste incinerators (HMIWI) are incinerators used by hospitals, health care facilities, and commercial waste disposal companies to burn hospital waste and/or medical/infectious waste. When burned, hospital waste and medical/infectious waste emit various air pollutants, including hydrochloric acid, dioxin/furan, and the toxic metals lead, cadmium, and mercury." "Air Regulations for Hospital/Medical/Infectious Waste Incinerators," Environmental Protection Agency Web site, last modified January 26, 2012, http://www.epa.gov/reg3artd/airregulations/ap22/incin2.htm.

The medical waste incinerator mentioned here is owned and operated by Stericycle. In a letter to the Florida Department of Environmental Protection dated October 28, 2010, Stericycle states, "Stericycle is the leading provider of compliant healthcare waste services to over 400,000 customers, including local health departments and public facilities. Within the state of Florida, Stericycle employs approximately 458 employees with 5 treatment facilities and 4 transportation facilities. Currently Stericycle operates 6 incineration treatment locations operating 8 incinerator units throughout the U.S., with one facility in Apopka, FL." Selin Hoboy, vice president of Legislative and Regulatory Affairs, Stericycle, Inc., to Lynn Scearce, rules coordinator, Florida Department of Environmental Protection, Division of Air Resource Management, http://www.dep.state.fl.us/air/rules/regulatory/hospital_waste/Steri_cycle_comments_10-28-10.pdf. In other words, the Stericycle plant in the South Apopka neighborhood incinerates waste from thousands of health care facilities throughout the country, not just from the local area or even just from Florida.

3. In fact, the case went to trial. "The situs of this case is the small city of Apopka, Florida, located in the fern and foliage growing region north of Orlando. More specifically, it is the poor, geographically separate, black community of that city. The plaintiffs . . . are a . . . class comprising the black residents of Apopka 'who are, or have been, subjected to the discriminatory provision of municipal services.' The main issues on appeal are whether the ongoing relative deprivation of the black community in the provision of municipal services

can lead to a finding of discriminatory intent sufficient to find a constitutional violation under the equal protection clause of the fourteenth amendment; whether the district court abused its discretion in impounding the federal revenue sharing funds of the City of Apopka; and whether the district court abused its discretion in the award of attorneys' fees. . . . Plaintiffs charged the City of Apopka, its mayor, and four council members with discrimination in the provision of seven municipal services: street paving and maintenance, storm water drainage, street lighting, fire protection, water distribution, sewerage facilities, and park and recreation facilities. After a preliminary finding by the Office of Revenue Sharing that the City was discriminatory in the provision of several of these services, an agreement was reached on improvements in street lighting and fire protection, and the district court filed an order settling these claims. The case went to trial on the remaining five issues." *Dowdell v. City of Apopka*, Florida, 698F.2d1181 (U.S. Ct. App. 11th Cir. 1983), http://scholar.google.com/scholar_case?case=2528468237629014219&q=698+f2d+1181&hl=en&as_sdt=2.

Chapter 7: "Learning the Hard Way"

1. "Medical waste is any solid or liquid waste which may present a threat of infection to humans, including nonliquid tissue, body parts, blood, blood products, and body fluids from humans and other primates; laboratory and veterinary wastes which contain human disease-causing agents; and discarded sharps. The following are also included: Used, absorbent materials saturated with blood, blood products, body fluids, or excretions or secretions contaminated with visible blood; and absorbent materials saturated with blood or blood products that have dried; and non-absorbent, disposable devices that have been contaminated with blood, body fluids, or secretions or excretions visibly contaminated with blood, but have not been treated by an approved method." "Florida Biomedical Waste," Gateway to State Resource Locators Web site, accessed September 25, 2013, http://www.envcap.org/statetools/rmw/fl-rmw.cfm.

2. "Biomedical Waste Program," Florida Department of Health Web site, last modified August 28, 2013, http://www.doh.state.fl.us/environment/community/biomedical/index.html.

3. Joel Abington, "Neighbors Wary of Incinerator Plan," *Baker County Press*, April 5, 2012, http://ufdcimages.uflib.ufl.edu/UF/00/02/41/60/00392/04-05-2012.pdf.

4. Kevin Spear, "Seeking New Landfill, Waste Company Offers Apopka $1M," *Orlando Sentinel*, October 13, 2011.

Chapter 8: "I Wish They'd Bring the Farms Back"

1. On the same day I learned this book was accepted for publication, I learned that Betty Lou Woods had passed away.

Chapter 10: "Education as the Way Out"

1. "The Future Directions of Lupus Research," U.S. Department of Health and Human Services, National Institutes of Health, and the National Institute of Arthritis and Musculoskeletal and Skin Diseases, August 2007, http://www.niams.nih.gov/about_us/Mission_and_Purpose/lupus_plan.pdf.

2. Jan Ehrman, "Pesticide Use Linked to Lupus, Rheumatoid Arthritis," *National Institutes of Health Record* 63, no. 6 (March 18, 2011), http://nihrecord.od.nih.gov/newsletters/2011/03_18_2011/story4.htm.

3. "An ANA test detects antinuclear antibodies in the blood. The immune system normally makes antibodies to help a body fight infection. In contrast, antinuclear antibodies often attack the body's own tissues—specifically targeting each cell's nucleus." "ANA Test," Mayo Clinic Web site, last modified August 31, 2011, http://www.mayoclinic.com/health/ana-test/MY00787.

Chapter 12: "Improving the Lives of Others"

1. "Vision & Mission," Farmworker Association of Florida Web site, accessed September 25, 2013, http://www.floridafarmworkers.org/index.php/about-us/vision-a-mission.

2. "The H-2A temporary foreign agricultural worker program allows agricultural employers to hire workers from other countries on temporary work permits to fill agricultural jobs that last ten months or less. To bring in H-2A guest workers, employers must first show that they have tried and are unable to find U.S. workers to meet their labor needs. Although the H-2A program includes some basic requirements to protect U.S. workers from negative effects on their wages and working conditions, as well as protect foreign workers from exploitation, it has been criticized for failing to protect vulnerable workers." "H2-A Guestworker Program," Farmworker Justice Web site, accessed September 25, 2013, http://farmworkerjustice.org/content/h-2a-guestworker-program.

3. In the early 1970s, Sisters Ann Kendrick, Cathy Gorman, and Gail Grimes, Roman Catholic nuns, formed the Office for Farmworker Ministry to work with the poor and neglected, specifically the farmworkers. They founded a farmworker credit union and a farmworker health clinic and organized farmworkers to empower them to struggle for better treatment and better living and working conditions.

4. "Agricultural workers are explicitly excluded from the protections of the *National Labor Relations Act* (NRLA), which gives most employees the right to engage in concerted activities for the purpose of mutual aid and protection.

Consequently, under Federal law, a farmworker may be fired for joining a labor union, and farm labor unions have no legal recourse to compel a company or agricultural employer to negotiate employment terms. The majority of state laws do not include any collective bargaining provisions for farmworkers." Bon Appétit Management Company Foundation, United Farm Workers, "Inventory of Farmworker Issues and Protections in the United States," iv, March 2011, http://www.bamco.com/uploads/documents/farmworkerinventory_0428_2011.pdf.

5. "Employers must comply with certain basic safety standards and regulations dictated by the *Federal Insecticide, Fungicide, and Rodenticide Act*. However, OSHA will not conduct inspections on farms with fewer than 11 employees unless states have memos of understanding with Federal offices to create their own rules. Pesticide exposure thus often goes undetected and/or unreported. Official pesticide data is inadequate for determining the actual extent to which farmworkers are exposed to these dangerous and often carcinogenic chemicals." Ibid., v.

Chapter 13: The Memorial Quilts

1. Her Web site is "that blackgirl art," http://www.thatblackgirlart.com.

Epilogue: View from the South Side

1. Spear, "Can Growing Hay on Dredged Muck Ease Lake Apopka Pollution?"
2. "The Lake Apopka North Shore Restoration Area (NSRA)," St. Johns River Water Management District Web site, accessed July 30, 2013, http://www.sjrwmd.com/lakeapopka/restoration.html.
3. "Orange County Wants to Save Lake Apopka Lands from Surplus Decision," Audubon of Florida News Blog, posted December 19, 2012, http://www.audubonoffloridanews.org/?p=12889.
4. "'Big 6' Guilty of Human Rights Violations," Pesticide Action Network North America Web site.
5. "What Is the Permanent People's Tribunal or PPT?" Permanent Peoples' Tribunal Web site, accessed September 25, 2013, http://www.agricorporateaccountability.net/en/page/ppt/2.
6. Permanent People's Tribunal, "Session on Agrochemical Transnational Corporations: Bangalore, 3–6 December 2011," 5, http://agricorporateaccountability.net/sites/default/files/tpp_bangalore3dec2011.pdf.
7. Indictment, Permanent Peoples Tribunal Session on Agrochemical Corporations, December 2011. Pesticide Action Network International, 194.
8. Ibid., 193.

Index

DALE FINLEY SLONGWHITE is a New Englander who transplanted a few years ago to Central Florida, where she learned of the Lake Apopka farmworkers. She is the founder-director of WriteLines (www.writelines.net), an organization offering creative writing workshops and retreats. She has published articles and essays in numerous magazines and newspapers and, with her sister, Sandra Finley Doran, is coauthor of the book *Gathering*.